ESSENTIALS FOR
HEALTH PROMOTION
IN NURSING

Carol A. Miller, MSN, RN-BC, is an independent care manager at Care & Counseling, where she focuses on promoting wellness for clients and their families. She has served many roles during several decades of her nursing career, including 2 years as a spokesperson for a national educational campaign about issues related to caregiving. Ms. Miller is author of *Nursing for Wellness in Older Adults 6e* (2012) and *Nurse's Toolbook for Promoting Wellness* (2007). *Nursing for Wellness* received the 1990 AJN Book of the Year Award in Gerontological Nursing and has been published in three foreign editions. Ms. Miller has published more than 100 nursing articles and textbook chapters. She has served as director of nursing, Cuyahoga County (OH) Nursing Home, and as nurse practitioner for the Cleveland Visiting Nurse Association. Ms. Miller has participated in several research projects, including one on Stresses and Supports in Caregiving (National Institute on Aging). Additional professional nursing roles include providing expert witness testimony related to nursing care of adults, serving as consultant to publishers, hospitals, nursing homes, and community agencies, and presenting at numerous national, state, and local conferences on many topics, including wellness. She has served on professional advisory boards and boards of directors for organizations such as Neighborhood Health Care and the Federation for Community Planning in Cleveland, Ohio.

19.7

OTHER E

Essentials for the NEW NURSE PRACTITIONER: What You Really Need to Know in a Nutshell (*Aktan*)

Essentials for the A&E NURSE: Emergency Department Orientation in a Nutshell (*Buettner*)

Essentials About GI AND LIVER DISEASES FOR NURSES: What APRNs Need to Know in a Nutshell (*Chaney*)

Essentials on COMBATTING NURSE BULLYING, INCIVILITY, AND WORKPLACE VIOLENCE: What Nurses Need to Know in a Nutshell (*Ciocco*)

Essentials for the THEATRE NURSE: An Orientation and Care Guide in a Nutshell (*Criscitelli*)

Essentials for the NEONATAL NURSE: A Nursing Orientation and Care Guide in a Nutshell (*Davidson*)

Essentials for the LONG-TERM CARE NURSE: What Nursing Home and Assisted Living Nurses Need to Know in a Nutshell (*Eliopoulos*)

Essentials for the CLINICAL NURSE MANAGER: Managing a Changing Workplace in a Nutshell (*Fry*)

Essentials for EVIDENCE-BASED PRACTICE: Implementing EBP in a Nutshell (*Godshall*)

Essentials for Nurses About HOME INFUSION THERAPY: The Expert's Best Practice Guide in a Nutshell (*Gorski*)

Essentials for MIDWIVES: Labour & Delivery Orientation in a Nutshell (*Groll*)

Essentials for the RADIOLOGY NURSE: An Orientation and Nursing Care Guide in a Nutshell (*Grossman*)

Essentials for the CARDIAC SURGERY NURSE: Caring for Cardiac Surgery Patients in a Nutshell (*Hodge*)

Essentials for DEMENTIA CARE: What Nurses Need to Know in a Nutshell (*Miller*)

Essentials for STROKE CARE NURSING: An Expert Guide in a Nutshell (*Morrison*)

Essentials for the PAEDIATRIC NURSE: An Orientation Guide in a Nutshell (*Rupert, Young*)

Essentials for the TRIAGE NURSE: An Orientation and Care Guide in a Nutshell (*Visser, Montejano, Grossman*)

Essentials for the HOSPICE NURSE: A Concise Guide to End-of-Life Care (*Wright*)

Essentials About PTSD: A Guide for Nurses and Other Health Care Professionals (*Adams*)

Essentials for the CLINICAL NURSING INSTRUCTOR: Clinical Teaching in a Nutshell (*Kan, Stabler-Haas*)

Essentials for MANAGING PATIENTS WITH A PSYCHIATRIC DISORDER: What RNs, NPs, and New Psych Nurses Need to Know (*Marshall*)

Essentials About the GYNAECOLOGIC EXAM: A Professional Guide for NPs, PAs, and Midwives (*Secor, Fantasia*)

Essentials for the CRITICAL CARE NURSE: Critical Care Nursing (*Landrum*)

Essentials of PRESSURE ULCER CARE FOR NURSES: How to Prevent, Detect, and Resolve Them (*Dziedzic*)

Essentials for HEALTH PROMOTION IN NURSING: Promoting Wellness (*Miller*)

Essentials of ADOLESCENT HEALTH FOR NURSING AND HEALTH PROFESSIONALS: A Care Guide (*Herrman*)

Essentials of EKGs FOR NURSES: The Rules of Identifying (*Landrum*)

Essentials for CURRICULUM DEVELOPMENT IN NURSING: How to Develop & Evaluate Educational Programmes (*McCoy*)

ESSENTIALS FOR HEALTH PROMOTION IN NURSING

Promoting Wellness

Carol A. Miller, MSN, RN-BC

SPRINGER PUBLISHING COMPANY
NEW YORK

Springer Publishing Company, LLC
11 West 42nd Street
New York, NY 10036
www.springerpub.com

Acquisitions Editor: Margaret Zuccarini
Composition: S4Carlisle

ISBN: 978-0-8261-3669-5

The author and the publisher of this Work have made every effort to use sources believed to be reliable to provide information that is accurate and compatible with the standards generally accepted at the time of publication. Because medical science is continually advancing, our knowledge base continues to expand. Therefore, as new information becomes available, changes in procedures become necessary. We recommend that the reader always consult current research and specific institutional policies before performing any clinical procedure. The author and publisher shall not be liable for any special, consequential, or exemplary damages resulting, in whole or in part, from the readers' use of, or reliance on, the information contained in this book. The publisher has no responsibility for the persistence or accuracy of URLs for external or third-party Internet websites referred to in this publication and does not guarantee that any content on such websites is, or will remain, accurate or appropriate.

Special discounts on bulk quantities of our books are available to corporations, professional associations, pharmaceutical companies, health care organizations, and other qualifying groups. If you are interested in a custom book, including chapters from more than one of our titles, we can provide that service as well.

For details, please contact:
Special Sales Department, Springer Publishing Company, LLC
11 West 42nd Street, 15th Floor, New York, NY 10036-8002
Phone: 877-687-7476 or 212-431-4370; Fax: 212-941-7842
E-mail: sales@springerpub.com

The ESSENTIALS series was published in the United States by Springer Publishing Company, LLC, as the FAST FACTS series.

Contents

Part III: Nursing Actions for Specific Aspects of Health Promotion

Preface

My interest in health promotion for wellness dates back to the community health nursing course I took during the senior year of my BSN program. I still have the paper I wrote on "The Creation of Health" in which I defined health as "a continual striving toward wholeness that can be reached only in relationship to our environment and the community of people around us." I had been inspired by Halbert Dunn's book *High-Level Wellness* and was enthusiastic—as well as idealistic—about applying these concepts as I cared for patients as a new nurse. My first job focused on geriatric and mental health patients, and I faced the significant challenge of meshing my ideals with the realities of my patient situations. During my years of nursing practice in various settings, I have increasingly appreciated that health promotion for wellness can be incorporated in any type of patient care situation by addressing needs holistically. As an independent care manager for more than 2 decades, I have many real-life opportunities to identify and implement actions that promote wellness for my clients and their caregivers. Several years ago, my skills and knowledge related to health promotion for wellness were validated when I became certified through the American Holistic Nurses Association. *Essentials for Health Promotion in Nursing: Promoting Wellness* represents the culmination of what I have learned and practiced about this topic since I first wrote about it as a nursing student.

Since Florence Nightingale, nurses have considered health promotion interventions as essential components of nursing care, and in recent years, health promotion has increasingly addressed broader aspects of body–mind–spirit connectedness. *Essentials for Health Promotion in Nursing: Promoting Wellness* summarizes much of the knowledge I have gained as I have researched, written about, and practiced the complex concepts associated with health promotion and wellness. More importantly, it applies this knowledge in an easy-to-use guide that nurses in adult health care settings can use to promote wellness for patients. I view health promotion for wellness as essential nursing actions that can readily be incorporated into usual care for patients under any circumstances. This book contains numerous tools to use for nursing assessment and as interventions, all based on a health promotion perspective. Because health promotion for wellness encompasses physical, mental, emotional, social, and spiritual aspects, the tools in the book can readily be used in any patient care situation to enhance well-being for patients. Perhaps most importantly, because healthy nurses provide optimal patient care, the tools can be applied for self-care to improve quality of life for nurses, both professionally and personally.

Chapters in Part I relate the concepts of health promotion and wellness to usual nursing care activities, with emphasis on strategies for teaching patients to promote wellness. Part II describes ways in which nurses promote wellness for all patients with regard to health protection, stress management, spiritual wellness, use of complementary and alternative medicine, nutritional wellness, and physical activity. The chapters in Part III provide tools for addressing health promotion in relation to the following topics: weight management and digestive wellness, cardiovascular wellness, respiratory wellness, urinary wellness, vision and hearing wellness, sexual wellness, and sleep wellness. Features that are unique to *Essentials for Health Promotion in Nursing: Promoting Wellness* are:

- *Essential Facts*: illustrate application of key concepts to clinical practice
- *Risk Assessment Tools*: identify risk factors that can be addressed in health promotion teaching
- *Wellness Assessment Guides*: provide assessment questions focused on health promotion
- *Wellness Teaching Tools*: summarize points for patient education
- *Wellness Activity Tools*: describe actions that can be used for health promotion
- *Self-Care in Practice*: brief prompts to encourage self-care for nurses

Carol A. Miller, MSN, RN-BC

Acknowledgments

First and foremost, I appreciate the multitude of ways in which my family, especially Pat Rehm, promotes my wellness, practically, emotionally, and spiritually—without their support and cheerleading it would be much more challenging to pursue my writing endeavors. I value the opportunities presented by teachers, clients, and colleagues that underpin my knowledge and practice of health promotion for wellness as a nurse. I also appreciate the support and assistance of all those at Springer Publishing Company, especially Margaret Zuccarini, who expertly guided this book through all its stages.

Principles of Health Promotion for Wellness in Nursing

Health Promotion and Wellness in Nursing

Health promotion has always been an essential component of nursing care, and the traditional approach has focused on screening for diseases such as cancer and on preventing communicable disease through immunizations. More recently, the scope of health promotion has expanded to focus on topics such as stress reduction, personal health responsibility, and interventions to prevent illness and improve health even when people feel healthy. Because of these trends, it is imperative that nurses address not only the more traditional aspects of health promotion but also those that are associated with patient wellness. Even though this topic is still evolving, there are many guidelines for health promotion for wellness that can be applied to nursing, as discussed throughout this book. This chapter sets the stage for applying these guidelines to nursing care.

In this chapter, you will learn:

1. Overview of health promotion for wellness
2. Incorporating health promotion for wellness during assessment
3. How to foster personal responsibility for wellness in patients
4. Practices for self-wellness for nurses

3

WHAT IS HEALTH PROMOTION FOR WELLNESS?

In 1893, Florence Nightingale answered the question of "What is health?" by stating, "Health is not only to be well, but to use well every power we have." She described the role of nurses as "helping the patient suffering from disease to live" and helping the healthy person "to have no disease" (Nightingale, 1893/1954). These reflections were written more than a century ago, but they are relevant to describing health promotion for wellness as it is addressed in this book:

- Health involves both the absence of disease and the use of personal power to achieve wellness, which is the ability to function at one's highest level, including physically, mentally, emotionally, socially, and spiritually.
- Wellness is a process that occurs one step at a time and is built on a foundation of personal responsibility.
- The role of nurses in health promotion for wellness is to assist patients in discovering where they are and where they want to be in this process, and to guide them in identifying and implementing the steps to achieve their wellness goals.

ESSENTIAL FACTS

The answer to *What is wellness?* is the statement *I'm OK and I want to be better.* Similarly, the answer to the question *How do nurses "do" health promotion for wellness?* is *You're OK and you can be better, and I can facilitate that process.*

HEALTH PROMOTION FOR WELLNESS IN PRACTICE

Despite the recognition that promoting wellness is an essential aspect of patient care, health care systems continue to emphasize efficiency, physical care, and use of technically advanced interventions. Nurses are challenged—and sometimes overwhelmed—by countless demands on their time, energy, and attention in clinical settings. In all clinical settings, the immediate priority is to address life-threatening and physical comfort needs. In the context of health promotion for wellness, another priority is to identify opportunities to address the broader needs of the whole person and his or her support people during the course of providing care.

People can work toward wellness at any time, whether they feel physically healthy or are dying, and personal wellness goals and choice of interventions will vary depending on health status, as in the following examples:

- Healthy people: prevention and early detection of disease, personal growth
- People with risks for disease: alleviation of risks
- People with chronic conditions: optimal management and daily functioning, prevention of decline or complications, mitigation of symptoms, especially pain or discomfort
- Patients experiencing acute illnesses: optimal management of physical, mental, emotional, and spiritual needs
- Patients recovering from serious illness: support to achieve optimal recovery
- Patients who have incurable and declining conditions: comfort and freedom from pain, support for addressing the many emotional and spiritual issues related to dying

======== *ESSENTIAL FACTS*

Because health promotion for wellness encompasses physical, mental, emotional, social, and spiritual aspects, it is possible to include at least one way to promote wellness in every clinical situation.

Health Promotion in Practice

Ms. T is in the coronary care unit recovering from coronary artery bypass surgery. Although she is alert and comfortable and her physical needs have been met, she seems anxious. You ask her if she is worried about anything and she says, "I am feeling closed in with all these tubes and the sound of machines all around—it feels like there's not enough air here." You take a minute to demonstrate a simple deep breathing exercise, you do it with her, and encourage her to do this frequently. This intervention alleviates her anxiety and provides her with a tool for self-care.

DEVELOPING A "WELLNESS WAY OF THINKING"

Health promotion for wellness is incorporated into usual patient care by applying a "wellness way of thinking" during nursing assessments and other nurse–patient interactions. This is not necessarily time consuming and can be accomplished by asking a relatively simple question while providing patient care. Examples of wellness-oriented questions are:

• Do you take time for any activities that are primarily for your wellness, rather than for addressing the needs of others?
• How often do you include self-wellness activities in your daily life?
• What do you do for self-wellness when you feel stressed?
• How does this situation affect your quality of life?

- What are your thoughts about things you could do when you feel anxious?
- How do you deal with your worries about the test results that will be back next week?
- What do you do for relaxation?
- Do you ever use simple breathing techniques for relaxation?
- Are there any relaxation techniques you would like some information about?
- Do you take time for enjoyable activities by yourself or with others?
- How does this affect your quality of life?
- How do you cope with feeling guilty about your mother having to go to a nursing home?
- Have you considered seeing a massage therapist?
- Are you familiar with using affirmations? . . . meditation? . . . guided imagery?

ESSENTIAL FACTS

Wellness-oriented nursing assessments depend more on the nurse's frame of reference than on the amount of time available.

Wellness in Practice

When a patient talks about a stressful situation, ask, "What do you do for self-wellness?" At a minimum, this simple question raises the patient's awareness about self-wellness, and it paves the way for supporting healthy behaviors and identifying stress reduction interventions.

PERSONAL RESPONSIBILITY AS THE FOUNDATION OF WELLNESS

Personal responsibility is the foundation of wellness because individuals, ultimately, choose between behaviors that affect their health positively or negatively. Personal responsibility for health is on a continuum that is influenced by both the patient and the type of intervention. At the minimal level, patients cooperate and accept interventions, such as medications and treatments administered by others. At a maximum level, patients initiate and participate fully in actions that are most beneficial and are supported by well-founded evidence of safety and efficacy. Nurses promote personal responsibility for wellness through interventions such as the following:

- Facilitating patients' self-awareness about their health
- Asking patients to perform a self-assessment of their current lifestyle to identify areas for improvement
- Discussing the relationship between behaviors and health
- Helping patients identify and address barriers to wellness-enhancing actions
- Helping patients develop an action plan to achieve positive health behaviors
- Informing patients about reliable sources of evidence-based information on which to base health-related decisions
- Teaching patients to use communication skills to discuss health care choices with their primary care practitioners and other health care providers
- Promoting responsible decisions regarding choices of interventions

ESSENTIAL FACTS

Patients may be basing health care decisions on misinformation about therapies that may not be safe or effective. Assess their understanding of so-called interventions and suggest sources of reliable information, such as the ones listed in ESSENTIAL RESOURCE in this book.

A major component of personal responsibility is awareness of one's current health status and the factors that affect one's health and functioning. Nurses facilitate patients' awareness of their health status and the factors that influence it by performing nursing assessments from a wellness perspective, as described in assessment guides in most chapters of this book. One way of assessing patients' perceptions about their health is by asking questions such as the following:

- On a scale of 1 to 10, with 1 being poor and 10 being very good, how would you rate your usual health during the past month?
- How has it changed—either better or worse—in recent years (or other time frame)?
- Does health affect your quality of life in undesirable ways?
- What conditions influence the way you feel, either positively or negatively?
- What would have to happen to improve your level of health?
- Have you identified any health-related goals for yourself?
- What conditions interfere with or support your efforts to achieve health-related goals?
- How much control do you feel over the conditions that have a negative effect on your health?
- Are you interested in finding out more information about steps you can take to improve your health?

ESSENTIAL FACTS

Questions about a patient's perception of health vary according to the clinical situation.

Health Promotion in Practice

In acute care settings, when asking about symptoms, include a question about the patient's typical level of health before the hospitalization. When caring for patients who have disabilities or chronic conditions, ask how their current level compares with their usual or optimal level of health and functioning.

Another aspect of developing personal responsibility is understanding that the goal of changing one's behaviors is to attain a higher level of health. People with chronic conditions usually develop an ongoing awareness of fluctuating levels of health and functioning. Similarly, people who recover from acute illnesses are usually aware of their variable experiences of health during and after these episodes. "Healthy" people, however, may not be aware of the importance of addressing conditions that increase the risk of disease. Health promotion for wellness focuses on teaching patients not only about interventions to address immediate needs but also about actions they can take to improve health. Often, these interventions involve motivation for behavior change, as discussed in Chapter 3.

ESSENTIAL FACTS

Help patients recognize the relationship between health and behaviors by asking how they feel after they engage in specific actions.

Health Promotion in Practice

Ms. B has knee pain intermittently, but it is becoming more chronic. You suggest that she keep a log of activities that positively or negatively affect comfort and functioning so this information can be used when planning interventions.

SELF-WELLNESS FOR NURSES

An unfortunate reality is that more than half of nurses who provide direct patient care in hospitals and nursing homes report feelings of burnout and job dissatisfaction (McHugh, Kutney-Lee, Cimiotti, Sloane, & Aiken, 2011). Typical signs of burnout in nurses are anger, frustration, fatigue, negativity, cynicism, withdrawal, and negative reactions toward others (Sabo, 2011). Even without burnout, however, nurses cope with myriad job-related stresses that are layered on stresses associated with all other aspects of their lives. Information and tools in this book are applicable not only to patient care settings but also to self-wellness for nurses. At the end of each chapter a brief feature called "Self-Wellness in Practice" illustrates how nurses can apply the information to promote wellness for themselves.

Health care organizations are addressing the need for stress management for nurses by offering training in interventions such as meditation, biofeedback, imagery, Reiki, and progressive muscle relaxation. Bormann and colleagues (2006, 2007) have developed and tested a simple and easy-to-use technique called Frequent Mantram Repetition, which has been used effectively for reducing stress in health care professionals and patient settings. HeartTouch is another easy-to-use technique developed and tested by a nurse that can be used to reduce stress in clinical settings (Walker, 2006). Nurses who practiced HeartTouch for 1 month noticed physical, mental, and emotional benefits for themselves, patients, colleagues, and family members (Walker, 2008). The following Wellness Activity Tools can be used to learn how to practice these self-care interventions. Videos illustrating how mantram has been effective in reducing stress for veterans with posttraumatic stress disorder are cited in the ESSENTIAL RESOURCES section.

Wellness Activity Tool:
Frequent Mantram Repetition

Frequent Mantram Repetition is a quick and easy technique that can be used at any time, in any situation, to focus attention and calm the body and mind.

Reasons for Using It

- It serves as a "rapid-focus tool" for the mind to interrupt automatic or negative thought patterns at any time or place.
- After repeating a mantram during calm periods, it becomes a "portable stress buster" when used to focus attention, slow thinking, and allow "pause time" for decision making.
- Clinical research studies (Bormann et al., 2006; Yong et al., 2011) have shown that mantram repetition can lower perceived stress, anxiety, and anger and can increase spiritual well-being in health care workers.

How to Choose a Mantram

- Choose a mantram (word or phrase with spiritual meaning) that has been repeated and shared for generations within all major faith traditions; don't make up your own.
- Examples of mantrams (and associated meanings) are:

Christian:	Maranatha (Lord of the Heart) or Jesus
Buddhist:	Om Mani Padme Hum (a blessing of the heart)
Hindu:	Rama (eternal joy within)
Jewish:	Shalom (peace)
Muslim:	Allah
Native American:	O Wakan Tanka (Oh, Great Spirit)

- Take your time and choose one that holds meaning for you and offers strength and support; it should be compatible with your spiritual beliefs; avoid words that have any negative associations.

- Use it for a few days or weeks to see how it feels; use it at night while falling asleep; change it if you feel you need to try a different one, but once selected, use it for the rest of your life.

How to Use a Mantram

- Practice repeating it quietly to yourself as often as possible, especially during nonstressed times (e.g., before going to sleep) so the mind–body connection is strengthened by associating it with a physiologic state of relaxation.
- Repeat it during times of distress or when dealing with feelings like anger or unwanted emotional states—each time it is used, it brings a stronger sense of calm and peace.

Developed by Jill E. Bormann, PhD, RN
Research Nurse Scientist
VA San Diego Healthcare System
Used with permission

Wellness Activity Tool: HeartTouch Technique

HeartTouch Technique is an internal method of helping nurses change their thoughts and feelings in order to positively affect their perceived stress and meaningful connections with self, others, and the Divine.

A. Heart-Centered Awareness

- Centering: Take three slow, deep breaths, focus your attention on your breath, let go of all distractions.
- Imagine a small circle of light in the center of your forehead and watch it move slowly down

your face, neck, and chest until it comes to rest over your heart. Allow the circle to grow with each inhale until it is a sphere encircling and permeating your entire chest area.

- Recall a time when you felt very loved or very loving toward another, whether person, animal, plant, or place. Relive the situation, feeling the feelings and experiencing it with all your senses, including any movement that was occurring.

B. Loving Touch

- Send the feeling of love to an individual by imagining it as a stream of light moving from your heart area to the heart area of the other. If you are touching the other in your mind or in reality, visualize the love as a stream of light moving down your arm to your hand, filling and surrounding the other individual.
- Mentally identify something about the other individual that you love and appreciate.

C. Connecting With Higher Power

- Finally, while maintaining the connection with the other individual, create a connection with whatever you perceive as a Higher Power, Source of Love, Light, Truth, and/or Wholeness, whether it be through prayers, meditation, or another personal method.
- Having created a connection with the other individual and a Higher Power, imagine a three-way connection between the individual, yourself, and a Higher Power, which might look like a triangle or circle of light.

- The feeling of love is the connecting energy between the nurse, the other individual, and Higher Power that creates balance, wholeness, and health.

Developed by Marsha Jelonek Walker, PhD, RN, AHN-BC, LMT
Used with permission

SELF-WELLNESS IN PRACTICE

Take a few minutes to carefully read the Wellness Activity Tool on Frequent Mantram Repetition or HeartTouch Technique and try one of these techniques now.

ESSENTIAL RESOURCES

Frequent Mantram Repetition Videos

Need to Know (PBS, June 22, 2012)
http://www.pbs.org/wnet/need-to-know/video/need-to-know-june-22-2012-homecoming-for-veterans/14098

YouTube (KPBS, April 3, 2012)
http://www.kpbs.org/news/2012/apr/03/vets-find-mantram-repetition-helps-ptsd-symptoms

2

Promotion of Wellness in
Patient Care Activities

As discussed in Chapter 1, developing a "wellness way of thinking" is a broad approach to incorporating health promotion for wellness while caring for patients. Actions to promote wellness are multifaceted but basically focus on addressing the holistic needs of patients as unique individuals. In addition, health promotion for wellness focuses on empowering patients toward personal responsibility for wellness.

In this chapter, you will learn:

1. Simple nursing interventions to empower patients for wellness
2. Principles of relationship-centered care
3. Relationship between cultural influences and patient care
4. Imagery as an easy-to-do intervention for promoting wellness

EMPOWERING PATIENTS

Because health promotion for wellness requires that patients actively participate in decisions about their health, patients and health care providers have a partnership relationship. Empowerment—defined as shared influence—is essential for achieving wellness because it facilitates knowledge about and motivation toward healthy choices. One way of empowering patients is by acknowledging them as partners during nursing assessments and interventions. In many circumstances, nurses assume the role of intermediaries between patients and other health care providers, and these situations provide opportunities to empower patients. For example, when several health care providers are involved with patients' care, nurses can explain the different roles and help patients formulate appropriate questions for different practitioners. Nursing actions to empower patients are described in relation to facilitating a sense of control, honoring each patient's individuality, and helping patients communicate with health care professionals, as in the following examples:

Facilitating a Sense of Control
- Involve patients in decisions affecting their health.
- Explain procedures before doing them.
- Allow choices about the timing of procedures, when possible.
- Ensure privacy as much as possible.
- Knock on doors before entering rooms.
- Ask patients their preferences about involving others in decisions about their care.
- If the patient prefers and as appropriate, arrange for trusted family or friend to participate in discussions about health issues.
- Make sure the patient has access to the assistive devices that improve his or her functioning (e.g., canes, walkers, eyeglasses, hearing aids, contact lenses).

Honoring Each Patient's Individuality
- Address patients by their preferred name and salutation.
- Recognize and affirm the unique cultural characteristics.
- Ask about the person's preferences and allow choices when possible.

Teaching Patients About Communicating
With Health Care Professionals
- Provide information, such as test results, when the information is within the realm of nursing practice.
- Help patients formulate and write questions to ask their primary care practitioner.
- Suggest reliable resources for self-education, in accordance with patient's ability to access these.

ESSENTIAL FACTS

Be aware of opportunities to empower patients who may not have a good understanding of their condition or treatment plan.

Health Promotion in Practice

Mrs. R has been admitted three times during the past year for congestive heart failure. When you review her discharge medications, she says, "My doctor told me to check my weight and take extra water pills if I eat too much, but every time I gain weight I end up in the hospital. I don't bother taking extra water pills because then I have to get up all night to use the bathroom." You teach Mrs. R about the role of diuretics in management of congestive heart failure and explain that the purpose of weighing herself is to monitor for fluid retention. You emphasize that Mrs. R can take an active role in preventing readmissions through the following actions: following her doctor's advice to monitor her weight and report weight gains, restricting dietary sodium, checking food labels for sodium content.

RELATIONSHIP-CENTERED CARE

The Institute of Medicine (2001) defined *patient-centered care* as being respectful and responsive to individual needs, values, and preferences. Health care settings now consider the concept of patient-centered care as an essential component of providing high-quality health care (Greene, Tuzzio, & Cherkin, 2012). A major emphasis of patient-centered care is the relationship between patients and their health care providers, with nurses playing an essential role. Health care professionals have developed a model of *relationship-centered care,* which is defined as "care in which all participants appreciate the importance of their relationships with one another" (Beach, Inui, & the Relationship-Centered Care Research Network, 2006, p. S3). This model is pertinent to all nurse–patient interactions, even when caring for patients in an environment that is not supportive of other principles of patient-centered care. The following principles of relationship-centered care can be applied in any care setting:

- Attending fully to the patient
- Promoting, accepting, and responding to the patient's emotions
- Showing empathy
- Appreciating the patient's understanding of his or her condition
- Respecting the person's own power and self-healing process
- Placing control with the person receiving the care
- Respecting each person's dignity, unity, and integrity
- Respecting each person's culture, experience, and perspective as valid and relevant to his or her care

- Viewing patients as experts and valuing patient–clinician partnerships as a therapeutic vehicle
- Establishing an ethic of love and service, beginning with self and extending to all relationships in the health care team

HONORING THE UNIQUENESS OF EACH PATIENT

Health promotion for wellness focuses on each patient as an individual who has a unique combination of needs. In this context, there is no place for stereotypes or preconceived ideas, and each person is approached within the context of his or her cultural identity. The concept of *cultural diversity* is used to distinguish a group based on any of the following identities: age, race, gender, language, ethnicity, occupation, physical size, religious practices, sexual orientation, political ideology, geographic location, and socioeconomic status. In reality, every aspect of every person's life is strongly influenced—both overtly and covertly—by cultural factors, but each person internalizes and maintains control over the impact of these influences. Thus, cultural background may strongly influence behaviors, but it does not determine who each person is as a unique individual. Rather than thinking in terms of respecting diversity or differences, a more holistic approach is to think in terms of honoring the uniqueness of each person because this approach emphasizes that there is no "cultural norm." Although general characteristics are likely to apply to a patient based on his or her cultural background or group identity, it is important to recognize that these generalizations may not apply to an individual group member.

ESSENTIAL FACTS

Even before providing care for patients, it is important to avoid judgmental perceptions that may be inaccurate or detrimental.

Health Promotion in Practice

If a patient's record states that he drinks four beers daily, we apply the information that is pertinent to his care, but filter out stereotypical images of him as an "alcoholic." Although we may decide to include additional questions about his drinking habits as we address his body–mind–spirit needs, we need to bring a nonjudgmental attitude to our communication with him.

Some cultural influences are inherited at birth, and others are acquired intentionally or unintentionally through life experiences. Some people make conscious efforts to learn about and experience other cultures so they can change and broaden their culturally based behaviors. Other people choose to maintain a strong and narrow focus and protect themselves from any influences that differ from their cultural heritage. Thus, some people are "multicultural" by virtue of being born to parents who have diverse cultural backgrounds, and others become multicultural as they identify with or get to know about a variety of groups. It is important to recognize that one's own cultural heritage and perceptions of cultural groups can influence interactions with others, and it may be necessary to make a conscious effort to override biases and honor the uniqueness of each patient. Questions such as the following can be used for self-reflection to identify cultural influences that can affect nursing care.

How Do I View Myself Culturally?

- What cultural heritage did I inherit at birth?
- What cultural group identities influenced me at different times in my life?
- How have I expanded my cultural group identities?
- What cultural group identities do I relate to now?
- What choices do I make about acknowledging or sharing information about my group identities?
- How has each of these groups influenced my beliefs and values?
- Do I feel any stigma or experience discrimination because I am associated with any cultural group?
- What do I like most and least about belonging to these groups?
- How does my sociocultural background influence my perceptions of concepts such as time, health, leisure, family, and relationships?

How Do I Perceive Others?

- How do I view people who were born in another country or speak a different primary language?
- What do I think about people who have the following characteristics: physically disabled, deaf or hard of hearing, grossly overweight, smokers?
- How do I view people who have tattoos, or body art, or piercings?
- What do I think about people who hold religious beliefs that differ from mine?
- How do I view people who dress very differently than those around them?
- Do I have difficulty relating to people who differ from me in their sexual orientation?

What Cultural Groups Do I Have Difficulty Relating To?

- How do I feel and respond when I have difficulty understanding others whose accents and primary language differ from my own?

========= *ESSENTIAL FACTS*

Not all cultural influences are obvious and some people try to conceal certain group identities. For example, individuals whose sexual orientation is gay, lesbian, bisexual, or transgender may be strongly influenced by their group identity but choose to hide their sexual orientation because of factors such as shame, discrimination, or fear of hate crimes.

COMMUNICATING WITH CULTURAL SENSITIVITY

An essential tool for honoring each patient's individuality is communicating with cultural sensitivity. This requires an awareness of verbal and nonverbal ways in which cultural diversity is communicated. The following is a guide to cultural influences on personal space, body language, and silence, with implications for nursing related to each type of nonverbal communication.

Personal Space (i.e., the range of territory in which a person is comfortable with others)
- Typical personal space zones in Western cultures: intimate is less than 1.5 ft, personal 1.5 to 4 ft, social 4 to 12 ft, and public more than 12 ft
- Groups likely to require a larger zone: British, Germans, Americans, Canadians, Scandinavians
- Groups likely to use a smaller zone: French, Africans, Japanese, Indonesians, Arab Muslims, Latin Americans

Implications for Nursing: Observe for indicators of patient's comfort zone, be aware of his or her response when providing care within the intimate zone, acknowledge the patient's response, and allow verbalization of feelings if the patient's personal space is threatened.

Touch
- Touching a person's head, shoulders, or hands (especially with the left hand) may be offensive in some cultures, but it is a sign of courtesy in other cultures.
- Touching done by people of the opposite sex may be considered taboo.
- Some cultural groups may prohibit male health care providers from touching or examining all or part of the female body.

Implications for Nursing: Be sensitive to patient perceptions of touch; identify culturally appropriate ways of touching patients during usual care activities (e.g., give medications to Arab Muslims in the right hand).

Facial Expressions and Body Language
- Direct eye contact may be viewed as aggressive and threatening.
- Some cultural groups avoid eye contact or cast their eyes downward as a sign of respect or an indicator of close attention.
- Smiling and hand gestures communicate many different feelings, including pain, happiness, displeasure, and aggression.
- A deep bow of the head and body is used to show respect, especially for a person from another cultural group.
- Crossing one's arms over the chest or crossing one's legs may be interpreted as a hostile act.

Implications for Nursing: Be aware of cultural variations in the meaning of nonverbal indicators, assess patients' responses to and use of nonverbal communication, use nonverbal communication purposefully and with cultural sensitivity.

Silence
- Recognize that some people cannot tolerate silence, and other people value it as a mode of communication.
- Presence can be an effective communication tool to encourage the expression of feeling.
- Silence can be viewed as an indicator of any of the following: agreement, respect and thoughtfulness, need for privacy, response to an inappropriate question.

Implications for Nursing: Identify effective ways of using silence when providing patient care; if appropriate, talk with patients about silence and give them permission to be quietly present to the situation.

PROMOTING PATIENT WELLNESS THROUGH SIMPLE NURSING INTERVENTIONS

Wellness Activity Tools throughout this book illustrate easy-to-implement nursing interventions to promote patient wellness. *Imagery* (also called *guided imagery*) is an example of an easy-to-do intervention that has been used as a body–mind intervention in many clinical settings. Studies have documented its effectiveness in all the following conditions: asthma, cancer, hypertension, fibromyalgia, migraine headaches, irritable bowel syndrome, anxiety and depression, immune system disorders, and posttraumatic stress disorder (Schaub & Burt, 2013). The following Wellness Activity Tool describes the use of imagery for health. The ESSENTIAL RESOURCES lists sources of additional information about imagery for health.

Wellness Activity Tool: Imagery for Health

Imagery is a mind–body intervention that is beneficial in many ways, including relaxation, stress reduction, alleviation of pain and fatigue, and improvements in energy and self-confidence. It takes only a few minutes and anyone can do it in any setting.

How to Do Imagery With Patients

Before you begin, clear your mind, take a deep breath, and focus on your breathing. Ask the patient if he or she would like to try a simple technique for relaxation and wellness. Ensure that the patient is positioned comfortably.

Direct the patient in the following process:

- Gently allow your eyes to close and bring your attention to the rise of your belly as you breathe in and to it settling in as you breathe out.
- Take a few minutes to appreciate the feeling of breath moving in and out.
- Now think of a favorite place where you feel safe and peaceful, or imagine a special time when you felt intense feelings of love and gratitude.
- Focus on all the ways this place [experience] feels real, using each of your senses. Guide the patient with phrases such as "look around at all the colors," "listen to the pleasant sounds," "notice the feel of the gentle breeze on your face," "allow the fragrant scents to fill your nostrils," "enjoy the delicious taste of your favorite treat."
- Imagine that you are surrounded by a cushion of loving energy so you feel safe and protected; then imagine that this cushion of energy is like a magnet drawing all the love and care that has ever been sent your way.
- Experience a profound feeling of wellness, knowing deep within that you are surrounded by love and protection.
- Now gather all these feelings and focus on your breathing.

- When you are ready to come back into the room, bring these feelings of love and protection, and know that you are better for this.

ESSENTIAL FACTS

In addition to using imagery in patient care settings, find opportunities to teach patients to use imagery.

Health Promotion in Practice

Mr. S is a dialysis patient waiting for a kidney donor. His emotional and spiritual needs are addressed through interventions such as encouraging him to verbalize feelings, assisting him in working through feelings such as anger, and validating his belief that he finds purpose in waiting for a kidney donor. In addition, you give him a copy of the Wellness Activity Tool and encourage him to use guided imagery designed specifically for people on dialysis, available at www.healthjourneys.com.

SELF-WELLNESS IN PRACTICE

Take a few minutes to practice using imagery to address a personal health concern, or simply to focus on your overall well-being.

ESSENTIAL RESOURCES

Academy for Guided Imagery
www.academyforguidedimagery.com

Healthjourneys (free 15-minute audio download on guided imagery for relaxation)
www.healthjourneys.com

3

Strategies for Teaching Patients
to Promote Wellness

Patient teaching has always been an important responsi-
bility of health care professionals, but the emphasis has
traditionally been on disease management rather than
on health promotion for wellness. In recent years, the fo-
cus has expanded to emphasize patient responsibility for
engaging in health-enhancing behaviors for preventing
or limiting the negative effects of disease conditions and
for promoting well-being of patients. Patient teaching re-
lated to health promotion can be as simple as teaching
about the recommended range for health measures (e.g.,
blood pressure, serum lipids, or body mass index) or as
complex as helping patients develop a plan for engaging
in behaviors to improve health or maintain an already
good level of health. As discussed in Chapter 2, patients
and health care professionals are partners and the role
of professionals is to guide patients in both discovering
their strengths and addressing their barriers so they
can incorporate healthy behaviors into their daily lives.
Chapters in Parts II and III of this book address patient
teaching in the context of specific aspects of functioning.
The focus of this chapter is on interventions that nurses
can use when they are helping patients change health-
related behaviors.

In this chapter, you will learn:

1. Positive models for patient teaching for health promotion
2. Communication skills to help patients develop healthy behaviors
3. How to use affirmations to promote healthy behaviors

POSITIVE MODELS OF BEHAVIOR CHANGE

In contrast to older models of behavior change that focus on problems to be solved, the current focus is on a positive approach that builds on patient strengths. Two positive models that nurses are using for promoting behavior change in patients are motivational interviewing and appreciative inquiry.

Motivational Interviewing

Motivational interviewing is an example of a positive model in which the health care professional assumes the role of a "change coach" and works collaboratively with the patient in a partnership relationship rather than in an authoritarian role. Key points in this model include:

- Honoring patient autonomy and self-direction
- Focusing on capacity rather than on incapacity
- Helping patients identify what they can do to make the changes, not on why they cannot change
- Using communication techniques of affirmation, summarizing, reflective listening, open-ended questions, and avoiding argumentation or direct persuasion
- Exploring questions about the patient's awareness of the problem, main concerns, intention to change, and confidence about changing
- Exploring goals and the costs and benefits of changing versus not changing

- Expressing empathy, caring, and a genuine interest in the patient's perspective
(Calhoun & Admire, 2005; Hancock, Davidson, Daly, Webber, & Chang, 2005)

Appreciative Inquiry

Appreciative inquiry is another affirmative model, which has been used since the 1980s in business settings and has recently been applied to promoting behavior change in health care settings. This model replaces deficit thinking with possibility thinking and uses a set of questions to appreciate and value the best of what is, envision a future of what might be, and dialogue about and create what will be. The process is divided into four steps designated as discover, dream, design, and delivery. Moore and Charvat (2007) propose that nurses use the appreciative inquiry approach to ask positive questions that explore the patient's experiences of what works or has worked to promote health. They suggest the following questions for each of the four steps:

- Discover: Describe a time when you had an exceptionally healthy lifestyle and consider the following questions: What did you appreciate about the experience? What was it about you that made this happen? What people or situational factors supported this positive experience?
- Dream: Imagine that you are so physically active that you feel very fit and healthy, and consider the following questions: What would you feel like on a daily basis? What would you be doing? How would you look? What would you be doing for exercise? How do you think it would help your heart?
- Design: What could you do now to be more in charge of your own health and care? Whom would you go to for help?
- Delivery: What are we going to do to start this process?

Through this dialogue, the nurse and patient engage in a cooperative search for strengths, passions, and life-giving forces so that the patient is open to new possibilities (Moore & Chavat, 2007).

=== *ESSENTIAL FACTS*

Recognize that many of the techniques that are outlined in motivational interviewing and appreciative inquiry are not unique to these models, but are "usual" communication methods commonly used by nurses.

NURSING SKILLS FOR HELPING PATIENTS DEVELOP HEALTHY BEHAVIORS

In addition to applying principles from behavior-change models, nurses apply many of their usual communication skills and interventions to help patients develop healthy behaviors. For example, the following nursing interventions are used to help patients increase healthy behaviors or decrease those that endanger their health: self-efficacy, values clarification, consciousness raising, restructuring, focusing on benefits, controlling the environment, counter-conditioning, and strengthening social support. The next paragraphs describe these interventions and provide examples of related communication techniques.

Improving self-efficacy: Increasing the patient's judgment that he or she is able to accomplish the desired behavior

- "Congratulations on your first week without cigarettes. I know it's hard work and you deserve a lot of credit for all your efforts. I'm sure your lungs appreciate it, and I appreciate the fact that there's less smoke in the air."

- "Give yourself credit for shedding those first 5 pounds— sometimes those are the hardest ones to lose, so you can be confident that you can keep making progress pound by pound."
- "Think about a time when you were successful in the face of a challenge, even though you weren't confident."
- "Describe a personal characteristic that helps you accomplish your goals."

Values clarification: Helping patients identify values in order to reconcile differences between expectations and behaviors

- "It's common to feel ambivalent about changing behaviors—you recognize that smoking, for example, increases the risks to your health but at the same time it's something that you enjoy doing. Let's talk about the ways in which your health is important to you."
- "It sounds like you have a conflict between believing that getting more exercise is good for your health and being concerned about not having enough time for it. Let's talk about how you can use your time to support your health."

Consciousness raising: Increasing patient's awareness about threats to health that are identified through routine assessments, screening and diagnostic tests, or risk appraisal tools (including self-assessments)

- "Your blood pressure has been around 156/90 for several weeks lately. Are you aware that the ideal range is below 120/80?"
- "Over the past 3 years your body mass index has shifted from normal range and is now in the overweight range; if this continues you will be in the obesity range by next year. People in that range are at increased risk for diabetes, especially if they also have high blood pressure, as you do."

Restructuring: Using positive thinking to focus on ways of overcoming barriers

- "I know it's very difficult to set aside time specifically for exercise, so let's try to identify some ways of getting more exercise during your usual activities. For instance, are there times that you could walk up and down stairs instead of taking an elevator?"
- "You've identified several things that get in the way of achieving your goal. Can you pick the one that is the easiest to tackle, and we'll see if we can find some ways to overcome that? I know that one of your strengths is facing your challenges, so let's look at one of those challenges and come up with a strategy that might work for you."

Focusing on benefits (also called reinforcing rewards): Immediately and frequently reinforcing benefits, which are classified as tangible, social, or self-generated

- "Let's focus on the benefits of quitting smoking. Do you know that within 1 day of quitting, your pulse rate and blood pressure improve and you've already decreased your risk for heart attack? Can you think of another benefit?"
- "Describe how you felt the last time you were at your ideal body weight."
- "Sometimes it helps to reward yourself for achieving short-term goals. What would be an appropriate reward for engaging in one-half hour of exercise for 4 days during the next week?"

Controlling the environment (also called stimulus control): Increasing cues that prompt desired behaviors and decreasing those that support undesirable behaviors

- "You said you find it easier to meditate when your children don't have the television on. Can you think of some ways to arrange things so you can have quiet time in the evenings when you want to meditate?"
- "You've identified beer, potato chips, and candy bars as foods that you find hard to resist. Let's talk about a plan for eliminating or controlling these temptations."

Counter-conditioning: Substituting healthy, pleasant behaviors for problem behaviors

- "You've identified that you eat more chocolate when you are stressed about your daughter, especially when she is out on a date. Can you think of a way to deal with your stress that doesn't involve food?"
- "You told me that when you are feeling overwhelmed at work, you spend your evenings and weekends reading a novel and you don't find that very satisfying. Can you think of an activity that could help you release some of the anxiety and at the same time provide healthy exercise?"

Strengthening social support: Involving family and friends in instructions, therapies, or values clarification

- "That's an excellent idea to walk with your friend for a half-hour during the time you usually talk on the phone."
- "You've told me you have so little time with your husband that you don't like to take the time to walk. Do you think he'd be willing to go walking with you at least once a week as sort of a 'date night'?"
- "Perhaps if you and your wife listen to the guided imagery together, you'll find it easier to do because it benefits both of you. Besides, the effects of guided imagery are strengthened when it's done with others."

ESSENTIAL FACTS

Self-efficacy can be addressed during patient teaching activities.

Health Promotion in Practice

When Ms. T reports that she keeps regaining weight soon after she loses it, the nurse responds, "So you have the ability to lose weight and you manage that well and often. You need to give yourself credit for that."

AFFIRMATIONS

Another intervention to help patients develop healthy behaviors is to teach about the influence of self-talk, which involves the messages we give ourselves that influence behaviors. *Affirmations*—which are strong, positive statements that reinforce important messages about a desired health state—are an easy-to-use method of fostering healthy behaviors. The following Wellness Activity Tool can be given to patients as a how-to guide about using affirmations for wellness.

Wellness Activity Tool: Affirmations

Affirmations are simple, strongly positive statements that can be used to change perceptions. Because thoughts influence actions, they can be used to support healthy behaviors as a sort of reprogramming to overcome negative thinking. Over time, they can have a profound, cumulative effect.

Affirmations for Meeting Health Goals
1. Identify a health-related goal and begin paying attention to your self-talk about barriers to

reaching your goal. For example, if your goal is to increase your level of physical activity, pay attention to your thoughts about the reasons you don't have time for this.

2. Develop a simple statement describing yourself taking the action or achieving your goal, as in these examples: I have 15 minutes every day for exercise, I am filled with energy for all I want to do today, I can lose weight, I can stop smoking, I am healthy in body, mind, and spirit.

3. State or write your affirmation at least 10 times daily for a month and think about this affirmation frequently during the day.

4. After a month, review your feelings about this affirmation and change or update it as needed.

Affirmations for Promoting Health

While breathing in deeply, read each statement in a state of open, relaxed attention; then breathe out while focusing on the message.

- I listen to my body and welcome the information it provides
- I eat foods that are good for me, and I avoid those that are unhealthy
- I frequently engage in enjoyable physical activities
- I am grateful for all my body does for me
- I pay attention to my needs and do what I can to address them
- I engage in healthy behaviors to nourish my body, mind, and spirit
- I frequently pause and pay attention to taking deep breaths
- I practice self-forgiveness

- I send kind thoughts to myself
- I appreciate that I can achieve a higher level of well-being

SELF-WELLNESS IN PRACTICE

Take a few minutes to carefully read the affirmations delineated in the Wellness Activity Tool, then develop two or three for yourself.

Strategies for Promoting Wellness
for All Patients

4

Teaching Patients to Protect Their Health

Health protection is an essential component of health promotion that focuses on preventive services, such as screening tests and immunizations, and self-care actions. Often this is an overlooked aspect of health promotion because actions need to be taken when people are healthy rather than in response to illness. Nurses have many opportunities to teach patients about actions they can take to protect their health.

In this chapter, you will learn:

1. Recommended preventive services for adults
2. Recommended adult vaccinations
3. Health-protecting actions in everyday life

PREVENTIVE CARE FOR ADULTS

The U.S. Preventive Services Task Force (USPSTF) is an independent panel of experts—including nurses, primary care practitioners, and health behavior specialists—that develops evidence-based recommendations related to preventive services. Recommendations are rated according to the strength of evidence from systematic research reviews. Recent recommendations of the USPSTF (2010) for preventive care with the highest rating of importance for adults are:

- Daily aspirin to prevent cardiovascular disease for men aged 45 to 79 and women aged 55 to 79 when the potential for disease prevention outweighs the risk for gastro-intestinal bleeding
- Blood pressure checks
- Tobacco use and counseling for all smokers
- Cervical cancer screening for sexually active women who have a cervix
- Screening for chlamydia in sexually active nonpregnant women who are aged 24 and younger or are at increased risk
- Screening for lipid abnormalities in men aged 35 and older and women aged 45 and older
- Colorectal cancer screening for all adults between the ages of 50 and 75 years
- Folic acid supplementation of 0.4 to 0.8 mg daily for all women who are capable of pregnancy
- For pregnant women: screening for bacteriuria and hepatitis B
- Screening for HIV for all adults at increased risk

Additional preventive interventions that are highly recommended but with a slightly lower rating of evidence are: screening and behavioral counseling to reduce alcohol misuse, breast cancer screening and counseling, depression screening, diabetes screening, nutrition counseling, obesity screening and counseling, and osteoporosis screening. Recommendations are also made for certain groups of adults, such as those who are pregnant, have a personal or family history of certain diseases, or engage in behaviors associated with health risks (e.g., smoking, drinking, unprotected sex). The USPSTF recommends that health care providers discuss all these services with adult patients as an integral part of usual care.

Health Disparities

In recent decades, health promotion programmes in the United States have substantially improved the health of residents. However, there is ongoing concern about health disparities, which occur most commonly in racial and ethnic minorities, people who do not have health insurance, and those who are poor and have less than a high school education. A recent report released by the Centers for Disease Control and Prevention (2011a) emphasizes that there are considerable and persistent gaps between the healthiest and least healthy people. For example, many racial and ethnic groups have higher rates of the following conditions that are amenable to preventive interventions: obesity, diabetes, hypertension, HIV/AIDS, and cervical cancer. Another disparity in preventive services is the significantly lower rates of adult immunizations among non-Hispanic Blacks and Hispanics.

ESSENTIAL FACTS

Although it is impossible to identify all risk factors for preventable and treatable conditions, it is important to address conditions that might warrant attention with regard to prevention and screening.

Wellness in Practice

Because Mrs. C's mother and sister are breast cancer survivors, you encourage her to ask her primary care practitioner about having screening tests at an earlier age than what is recommended for the general population.

Promoting Personal Responsibility for Preventive Care

An important aspect of health promotion for wellness is teaching patients about preventive interventions that are applicable to their situation. The following Wellness Activity Tool summarizes evidence-based recommendations for men and women, with emphasis on preventive practices that are the most cost effective, consistently supported by research, and applicable to the general population. Organizations listed in the ESSENTIAL RESOURCES at the end of this chapter provide downloadable and interactive tools for use by patients and professionals to identify preventive practices applicable to individual situations.

Wellness Activity Tool: Guide to Protecting Health for Adults

Practice Healthy Behaviors
- Be tobacco free
- Be physically active

- Eat a healthy diet
- Maintain a healthy weight
- Drink alcohol only in moderation
- Get a flu shot every year
- Keep up to date on recommended vaccinations, including pneumonia and herpes zoster
- Talk with your primary care practitioner about daily aspirin: men starting at age 45 and women starting at age 55, or younger with risk factors

Recommended Screenings for All Adults
- Body mass index (BMI) (calculator available at www.nhlbisupport.com/bmi)
- Blood pressure at least every 2 years starting at age 18
- Cholesterol, starting at age 20 for women and 35 for men or earlier if you have risk factors
- Colorectal cancer, starting at age 50 or earlier with a family history
- Diabetes if you have high blood pressure or high cholesterol
- Sexually transmitted infections if you are sexually active with more than one partner
- HIV if you have risks
- Depression if during the past 2 weeks you have felt sad, down, or hopeless or if you felt little interest or pleasure in doing things

Men Only
- Abdominal aortic aneurysm if you are between the ages of 65 and 75 years and have smoked

Women Only
- Mammogram
- Pap smear every 1 to 3 years between the ages of 21 and 65, unless you do not have a cervix
- Osteoporosis starting at age 65 or younger if you have risk factors
- Chlamydia if you are 24 years or younger and sexually active

Source: www.ahrq.gov/ppip/healthywom.htm and www.ahrq.gov/ppip/healthymen.htm

PROMOTING ADULT IMMUNIZATIONS

Despite a plethora of evidence that vaccines are a successful and cost-effective public health measure, adult immunizations are often overlooked as a health protection intervention. The National Immunization Program of the Centers for Disease Control and Prevention emphasizes that adult immunizations are an essential aspect of health promotion for adults for all of the following reasons:

- Some adults were never vaccinated as children.
- Newer vaccines were not available when some adults were children.
- Immunity can begin to fade over time.
- Increased age increases susceptibility to serious disease caused by common infections (e.g., flu, pneumonia, tetanus, and diphtheria).

The following Wellness Teaching Tool summarizes current recommendations of the Centers for Disease Control for adult immunizations.

Wellness Teaching Tool:
Recommended Adult Vaccinations

Adult Vaccinations	Recommendation
Hepatitis A	People who have chronic liver disease or conditions requiring the use of blood products; illegal drug users; men who have sex with men; and people who are exposed to or at risk of exposure to hepatitis A
Hepatitis B	People who have the following risk factors: dialysis, chronic liver or kidney disease, diabetes if under age 60 years, exposure to human blood or other body fluids, illegal drug use, risk of exposure to hepatitis B through sex partners, occupation, or travel
Human papillomavirus (HPV)	Previously unvaccinated men through age 21 and women through age 26; men through age 26 if they have sex with men or are immunocompromised
Influenza	All adults every year before the beginning of flu season

Meningococcal disease	College students through age 21 years who live in residence halls; people who travel or reside in countries where meningococcal disease is common
Pneumonia	One-time dose for people aged 65 years and older and those who have risk factors such as smoking, chronic conditions, alcoholism, immunocompromised status
Tetanus, diphtheria, pertussis	Primary series, then booster every 10 years for all adults, especially after sustaining a puncture wound (tetanus)
Varicella (chickenpox)	Two doses for adults who do not have evidence of immunity

PROMOTING HEALTH PROTECTION IN EVERYDAY LIFE

An important, but often overlooked, aspect of health promotion is reminding patients about simple actions they can take to protect their health in everyday life. The following Wellness Activity Tool can be given to patients to teach about many simple actions they can incorporate in routine activities to protect their health. Chapters in Part III discuss additional health-protecting actions and provide details about the actions in this tool.

Wellness Activity Tool: Simple Health-Protecting Actions for Everyday Life

Health-Protecting Actions	Positive Health Effects
Wear protective clothing and use sunscreen with SPF of at least 15 when exposed to sunlight; for extended outdoor activity, use sunscreen with 30 SPF or higher and reapply frequently	Prevention of skin cancer and wrinkles
Use good oral care practices, including brushing and flossing of teeth and getting regular dental check-ups	Prevention of tooth loss, dental caries, and gum disease
Wear sunglasses when exposed to sunlight, get eye exams starting at age 40	Prevention and early detection of eye disease
Avoid exposure to loud noise and wear ear protectors when noise cannot be avoided	Prevention of noise-induced hearing loss
Not smoking, maintaining heart-healthy dietary intake, exercising regularly, and using effective stress management methods	Prevention of cardiovascular disease
Not smoking, avoiding exposure to second-hand smoke and other pollutants, wearing a protective mask when exposed to dust and harmful air-borne particles	Protection from respiratory disorders

Engaging in regular physical activity, wearing supportive shoes, using caution to prevent falls	Prevention of musculoskeletal injuries
Washing hands frequently, using precautions when around people with colds and other infections, keeping up to date on annual flu immunizations	Protection from communicable diseases
Using seat belts when riding in vehicles, wearing helmet when riding bicycle or motorcycle, using protective eye goggles when appropriate, taking precautions to avoid falls, having smoke and carbon monoxide detectors in appropriate places in the home	Protection from serious injuries

ESSENTIAL FACTS

Patients are more likely to engage in relatively easy health-protecting actions when they are reminded about the positive effects of their actions.

Wellness in Practice

Nurses can teach about the benefits of simple health-protecting actions such as using helmets, sunglasses, sunscreen, seat belts, ear protectors, safety goggles, and athletic protectors.

SELF-WELLNESS IN PRACTICE

Take time for a self-assessment of your health protection needs by using the interactive tools for adult immunizations and screening tests that are available at www.cdc.gov/features/adultimmunizations and www.healthfinder.gov/prevention.Print the results for your personal health care record and discuss pertinent needs with your primary care practitioner.

ESSENTIAL RESOURCES

Agency for Healthcare Research and Quality
www.ahrq.gov

Centers for Disease Control and Prevention
www.cdc.gov

Quick Guide to Healthy Living
www.healthfinder.gov/prevention

U.S. Preventive Services Task Force
www.uspreventiveservicestaskforce.org

5

Stress Management

Helping patients manage stress is an essential component of health promotion because of the serious and persistent impact of chronic stress on health. Patients may not be aware of the relationship between chronic stress and health, and they may even perceive stress as a "normal" part of everyday life rather than as something that requires a conscious response. Information in this chapter is applicable not only to many, if not all, patient care situations but also to self-wellness in daily life.

In this chapter, you will learn:

1. How stress affects health and is pertinent to health promotion
2. Characteristics of acute and chronic stress
3. How to assess stress and coping in patients
4. Interventions to reduce stress in patient care situations
5. How to teach patients about stress management and meditation

THE RELATIONSHIP BETWEEN STRESS AND HEALTH

Our understanding of the relationship between stress and health has evolved considerably since the 1920s when the phrase *fight or flight response* was used to describe the predictable physiologic reaction that is stimulated by fear or other stressors in response to an external stimuli. Fifty years later, Hans Selye (1974) expanded this concept and described the *stress response* (also called the *general adaptation syndrome*), which included the following stages:

- Perception of a physical or emotional stressor
- Autonomic nervous system response to prepare for fight or flight (alarm stage)
- Physiologic adaptation to stressor and return to homeostasis (resistance stage)
- Exhaustion stage, in which the body either rests or reaches total exhaustion and dies

Current understanding of stress distinguishes the effects of the fight or flight response—which is helpful in acute situations—and chronic stress, which stimulates a different physiologic response involving the endocrine and immune systems as well as the nervous system. Table 5.1 describes distinguishing features of acute and chronic stress.

Effects of Stress on Health

It is now well understood that chronic stress suppresses immune function and leads to an inflammatory response that

TABLE 5.1 Distinguishing Features of Acute and Chronic Stress

Feature	Acute Stress	Chronic Stress
Type of stressor	Threatening, unexpected, uncontrollable, unfamiliar	Conditions that are perceived as stressful and last for more than several days; acute stresses that do not resolve quickly; major life events, including happy ones (e.g., weddings, births, career changes)
Examples of stressor	Injury, loss of job, sudden onset of pain, illness, major traffic jam, hospitalization for oneself or family member, invasive or painful medical procedures	Serious illness or disability, social or occupational relationship issues, financial strains, joblessness, unresolved conflicts, abusive or dysfunctional relationships, loss of close relationship
Physiologic response	Increased heart and respiratory rates, sweating, shortness of breath, decreased digestive enzymes	Chronic release of stress hormones, diminished levels of cortisol, compromised immune function, increased susceptibility to acute and chronic illnesses
Effects	Can be positive, beneficial, motivating, and even lifesaving when action is taken to resolve the threat	Cumulative negative effects on health: increased incidence of cancer, diabetes, hypertension, infections, tension headache, cardiovascular disease, gastrointestinal disorders, low back pain, poor wound healing, postsurgical complications
Level of awareness	Readily recognized because the stressor and response occur in a short time	May be subtle and unrecognized because the situation evolves gradually and becomes long term
Management approaches	Resolve the stressful situation by taking action, use deep breathing techniques and other relaxation methods if not in immediate danger	Counseling and support groups; regular participation in relaxation techniques (e.g., deep breathing, yoga, meditation, guided imagery); healthy lifestyle practices (e.g., good nutrition, regular physical activity)

can trigger many illnesses. Studies indicate that effects of chronic stress are directly linked to the following conditions:

- Upper respiratory infection (i.e., common cold) (Cohen et al., 2012)
- Coronary artery disease (Ho, Neo, Chua, Cheak, & Mak, 2010)
- Inflammatory bowel disease (Mackner, Clough-Paabo, Pajer, Lourie, & Crandall, 2011)
- Fatigue (Silverman, Helm, Nater, Marques, & Sternberg, 2010)
- Depression (Blume, Douglas, & Evans, 2011)
- Delayed wound healing (Gouin & Kiecolt-Glaser, 2011)
- Dermatitis (Suarez, Feramisco, Koo, & Steinhoff, 2012)
- Multiple sclerosis (Sorenson, Janusek, & Mathews, 2011)
- Psoriasis (Evers et al., 2010)

ESSENTIAL FACTS

Recognize that stress is a normal response to any major change, including those that are wanted and intentional (e.g., births, vacations, weddings, promotions, graduations, new relationships).

Health Promotion in Practice

When you assess Mrs. V, she reports that she returned yesterday from a "wonderful family vacation" and is experiencing a major flare-up of her usually well-controlled rheumatoid arthritis. She is concerned that her usually well-controlled condition has "taken a turn for the worse." When you ask additional questions about stress, Mrs. V recognizes that she was much more physically active than usual during vacation, and she agrees that if she still feels this way after she gets back to her "baseline" she will make an appointment with her rheumatologist.

ASSESSING PATIENTS' STRESS AND COPING

An integral part of promoting wellness for patients is asking about sources of stress as well as usual ways of coping. When asking about coping strategies, identify constructive methods that the patient is familiar with so these can be supported and ask about the patient's willingness to learn new methods. Also, check for indications—or ask directly if appropriate—about unhealthy coping mechanisms, such as smoking, over-eating, excessive drinking, use of illegal drugs, or engagement in violent or risky behaviors.

=========================== *ESSENTIAL FACTS*

During usual interactions with patients there are many opportunities to discuss their experiences of stressful situations and set the stage for teaching about effective ways of managing stress.

Health Promotion in Practice

You are caring for Mr. D when his cardiologist visits to inform him that he will not be able to return to his construction job for a while, but he can participate in an outpatient cardiac rehabilitation clinic. After the doctor leaves, he states, "The only rehab I need is to get back to work where I can let off steam with my buddies." You ask if he has other ways of coping with stress and you tell him that one of the main advantages of the cardiac rehab program is that he will learn stress management techniques.

GUIDE FOR ASSESSING STRESS AND COPING

Observe for Indicators of Acute Stress

- Increased pulse, respirations, and blood pressure
- Sweating, tremors, rapid breathing, dry mouth, urinary frequency
- Fearful facial expressions
- Increased muscle tension
- Behaviors such as pacing, restlessness, repetitive movements
- Complaints of headache, backache, gastrointestinal symptoms

Ask About Sources of Chronic Stress

- What major changes have you experienced recently?
- Have you experienced any major losses (e.g., deaths of family, friends, significant others; separations due to relocation or disputes with family or friends; loss of pets; loss of property due to disasters)?
- What circumstances in your life are sources of worry?
- What circumstances in your life are sources of emotional satisfaction or positive stress?

Ask About the Patient's Experience of Stress

- What physical symptoms and emotional responses do you experience when you are stressed?
- Are there times that stress affects your ability to engage in your usual energy or activities?
- Are there times that stress affects the management of your _____ (e.g., diabetes, arthritis, fibromyalgia)?

Ask About Coping Strategies

• What do you do to cope when you feel _____ (stressed, worried, anxious)?
• Whom do you turn to for support when you feel stressed?
• Are there coping strategies that you feel are effective but you no longer do (e.g., meditation, getting physical exercise)?
• Are there ways you use to deal with stress that you would like to change?

NURSING ACTIONS TO HELP PATIENTS MANAGE STRESS

When caring for patients, nurses have many opportunities to implement relatively simple interventions for addressing stress, as in the following examples:

• Touching appropriately in a calm and caring manner
• Engaging the patient in a brief deep-breathing exercise
• Addressing physical needs in a timely manner (e.g., pain, thirst, hunger, positioning, elimination)
• Facilitating optimal level of functioning (e.g., easy access to their eyeglasses and assistive devices)
• Adjusting the environment for quiet, comfort, and privacy
• Making sure that phones, call bells, and remote controls are within reach
• Providing information to patients
• Communicating respect for the patient's individuality
• Involving the patient in planning his or her care
• Facilitating the exchange of information among all care providers
• Providing any nursing actions that reduce stress in acute care settings

ESSENTIAL FACTS

During usual care activities, take a second to ask patients if they are willing to try a stress reduction method (or "comfort measure"), such as breathing for relaxation.

Health Promotion in Practice

When you administer medications to Mrs. A, you notice that she has been crying and she tells you she's very upset about what the doctor told her. You ask her to tell you more about what the doctor said and you express empathy. You then say, "I'm sure this is a very stressful time for you; I'd like to show you a simple deep breathing exercise that's good for releasing tension. Close your mouth and take a very deep breath through your nose, expanding your belly as much as you can, then open your mouth and exhale fully." You demonstrate the technique and ask her to do it with you—this helps both you and the patient release stress.

Teaching Patients to Manage Stress

A key intervention for helping patients manage stress is teaching them to identify types of stress and develop effective coping strategies for use in daily life. The following Wellness Activity Tool can be used as a patient handout or as a guide for discussing stress management in daily life. Wellness Activity Tools in other chapters also can be used to teach about specific stress management techniques, as in the following examples: Mantram repetition (Chapter 1), affirmations and imagery (Chapters 2 and 3), aromatherapy (Chapter 7), and physical activity (Chapter 9).

Wellness Activity Tool:
Tips on Managing Stress in Daily Life

Recognize the Different Types of Stressors
- Events are stressful according to the degree to which they have an emotional impact and are perceived as desirable and controllable.
- It is important to manage your responses to stressful events, even when the stress cannot be alleviated.
- Different coping mechanisms are effective for different types of situations: emotion-focused strategies are best for situations that cannot be changed, and problem-focused strategies are useful for situations that can be changed.

Coping Strategies for Situations That Cannot Be Changed
- Develop an attitude of acceptance, reframe your perspective, and focus on what you can learn from this.
- Acknowledge and express feelings, even those that are unpleasant, such as grief, anger, and sadness.
- Talk with someone and accept that person's caring and understanding; communicate to that person that you do not expect to change the situation but appreciate an opportunity to express feelings.
- Foster supports for social, emotional, and spiritual enrichment (e.g., friends, family, pets, hobbies, groups).
- Identify and use healthy ways of releasing tension and expressing emotions (e.g., physical activity, actions that lead to a sense of accomplishment).

- Engage in distracting activities, especially those that are pleasurable, health enhancing, and spiritually enriching.
- Use relaxation methods, such as meditation, yoga, progressive relaxation.
- Express feelings and develop insights through activities such as journaling and self-talk.
- Seek guidance from counselors or health care professionals.

Problem-Focused Coping Strategies

- Time pressures: Evaluate demands, determine priorities, and plan a schedule for the most important things, including time for activities that relieve stress.
- Set realistic limits and become comfortable telling others what they are.
- Seek advice and reliable information from friends, family, or professionals who can assist with developing a problem-solving plan.
- Adapt the environment so it is most conducive to your current needs.

Strategies to Avoid

- Smoking
- Excessive eating or drinking (including alcohol or caffeine)
- Inappropriate use of medications or recreational drugs
- Inaccurately or inappropriately directing anger or emotions toward others
- Actions that are harmful to people, animals, or the environment

≡ *ESSENTIAL FACTS*

Caregiver stress and posttraumatic stress disorder are two types of stress syndromes that nurses can address by suggesting referrals for widely available support groups.

MEDITATION

Meditation is a mind–body practice that has many physiologic effects, including the ability to activate the autonomic nervous system (National Center for Complementary and Alternative Medicine [NCCAM], 2010). Studies have documented behavioral outcomes (e.g., improvements in anxiety, insomnia, depression, and quality of life) as well as positive physiologic effects on the immune and neurologic systems (Kreitzer & Reilly-Spong, 2010). Meditation is often recommended as a complementary therapy for conditions such as anxiety, depression, stress reduction, hypertension, cardiovascular disease, and many chronic illnesses.

A confusing array of labels is applied to meditation, but all definitions include the act of clearing one's mind to focus on an image or thought. Commonly used terms and associated descriptors include the following:

- *Relaxation Response Meditation*, developed by Herbert Benson and his Harvard colleagues during the 1960s, involves a quiet environment, a comfortable position, a mental device (i.e., a single syllable sound or word), and a passive attitude.
- *Transcendental Meditation,* developed in the early 1960s by the Indian leader Maharishi Mahesh Yogi, involves the repetition of a mantra (sound or word) while seated in a comfortable position.

- *Mindfulness-Based Meditation*, based on Buddhism and developed by Jon Kabat-Zin in the 1970s, emphasizes the concept of being mindful, or having an increased awareness and total acceptance of the present.
- *Centering Prayer*, developed during the 1990s as a discipline to focus attention on union with God, involves finding a comfortable position and focusing on a sacred word.
- *Moving Meditation* is a term applied to relaxation methods that involve focused attention and body movements (e.g., yoga, qi gong, chi kung, tai chi).

The following Wellness Activity Tool describes the use of meditation as a stress reduction intervention. It is important to emphasize that a variety of meditation techniques are promoted but there is no single method that is best for everyone.

Wellness Activity Tool: Meditation

Meditation is an easy-to-use self-care practice for relaxation, stress management, and overall wellness. Meditation can be done in many ways and in different positions, but all types share the following elements: clearing one's mind, focusing attention, and being in a quiet location and relaxed state.

General Guidelines
- Don't worry about following a "recipe" for a specific technique—try different ones and develop a method that works well for you.
- Commit to making meditation a daily health care practice—view it as an essential health-related activity, just like good nutrition and regular physical activity.
- Try to start and end your day with meditation, using different methods for the morning and evening.

- Begin with 5-minute sessions twice daily and gradually work up to 20 to 30 minutes each time (set a timer if that is helpful).

How to Do: Still-Position Meditation
- Find a quiet location and position yourself comfortably with your back straight, usually either lying down or sitting in a chair with your feet on the floor.
- Gently close your eyes and relax.
- Breath slowly and deeply by fully expanding and contracting your belly for inspirations and expirations.
- Focus your attention on your breathing and experience the flow of air as it enters and leaves your nostrils.
- If your attention wanders, bring it back by focusing on your breathing.
- Continue focusing your attention on your breathing.
- Mentally scan your body and breathe relaxation into each part on the inhalations, and release stress from each part on the exhalations.

How to Do: Walking Meditation
- Find a location that is conducive to relaxation for you (it can be inside or outside).
- Begin by clearing your mind and focusing your attention on slow and deep breaths.
- Establish a personal ritual to indicate the beginning of your walking meditation (e.g., stand still, close your eyes, scan your body, and ask your feet for good support).
- As you walk, focus your attention on the movement of your feet and the support of the ground.
- Experience a sense of connectedness to the earth with each step.

- Mentally scan your body and appreciate the rhythmic movements of each part.
- If your attention wanders, bring it back by focusing on your rhythmic movements.
- Engage in a personal ritual to indicate the end of the meditation (e.g., stand still, scan your body again, and thank your feet for helping you on your brief meditation journey).

SELF-WELLNESS IN PRACTICE

Use an interactive stress self-test at one of the following websites and consider recommending it for patients to try: Stress screener at www.mentalhealthamerica.net/llw/stressquiz.html; test your stress smarts at www.apa.org/helpcenter/stress-smarts.aspx; or Stress-o-meter at www.bam.gov/sub_yourlife_stressometer.html

ESSENTIAL RESOURCES

American Academy of Dermatology, Stress and Skin
www.aad.org
American Heart Association, Stress Management
www.heart.org
American Psychological Association
www.apa.org/helpcenter
National Cancer Institute
www.cancer.gov/cancertopics/factsheet/Risk/stress
National Center on Complementary and Alternative Medicine
http://nccam.nih.gov
National Institute of Mental Health
http://nimh.nih.gov
Quick Guide to Healthy Living, Managing Stress
www.healthfinder.gov/prevention

6

Spiritual Wellness

Since the time of Florence Nightingale, nurses have recognized that they address the spiritual needs of their patients, but this still remains one of the most nebulous aspects of nursing care. When asked about providing spiritual care, most nurses know that they "do it," but they have difficulty describing what "it" is. Even though major nursing and health care organizations emphasize the importance of nurses addressing the spiritual needs of patients, assessment questions are usually limited to obtaining information about a patient's religious affiliation. Similarly, interventions often focus on initiating referrals to chaplains or other spiritual advisors for patients who have a religious affiliation. This approach may be adequate for some patient care situations, but it does not necessarily address the need for a spiritual connectedness that all humans experience. This chapter focuses on relatively simple actions that nurses can incorporate as an integral part of usual nursing care to identify and address the spiritual needs of their patients.

In this chapter, you will learn:

1. Relationship of religion and spirituality to health promotion
2. Roles of nurses in promoting spiritual wellness for patients
3. How to assess the spiritual needs of patients
4. Nursing actions to promote spiritual wellness: listening, presence, prayer, and fostering spiritual practices

RELIGION, SPIRITUALITY, HEALTH, AND NURSING

Religion and spirituality are closely related terms, but they can be differentiated in the following ways:

- *Religion* refers to an organized system of spiritual beliefs and practices shared by a group of people; as such, it provides specific ways of expressing one's spirituality for some people. Examples of religious practices include ritual, worship, dietary observances.
- *Spirituality* is a universal human experience that encompasses one's sense of connectedness with self, others, nature, and a spiritual being (e.g., God, Divine, Higher Power). Examples of spiritual practices include yoga, meditation, creative activities, meaningful relationships, experiences of nature.
- Both religion and spirituality affect health beliefs and practices (e.g., provision of social supports, selection of practitioners and treatments).

There is much agreement that religious and spiritual practices can have many beneficial effects on health, such as better health behaviors, improved immune function, quicker recovery from illness, and lower rates of diseases. For example, studies have shown that meditation can improve health-related outcomes in all the following conditions: anxiety, asthma, cancer, chronic pain, coronary artery disease, depression, fibromyalgia, HIV/AIDS, hypertension, irritable bowel syndrome, menopause, psoriasis, posttraumatic stress disorder, and sleep disturbance (Kreitzer & Reilly-Spong, 2010). Thus, it is important to view spirituality as an important component of health promotion for all patients.

Another nursing responsibility is to address needs of patients who are experiencing spiritual distress, for example, during times of serious threats to their health or life. Patients who are experiencing spiritual distress may express feelings of hopelessness, alienation, guilt, need for forgiveness, and anger toward God. Even in the absence of spiritual distress, however, nurses can address spiritual needs as a routine part of holistic care.

ESSENTIAL FACTS

It is important to become comfortable discussing spiritual needs of patients because all humans have spiritual needs even though they may not identify with a religion.

Health Promotion in Practice

You are a nurse working in a Catholic hospital, but you feel uncomfortable discussing religion because you do not have any religious affiliation. You address your discomfort by reminding yourself of the many spiritual practices you engage in and by developing an inquisitive and open-minded approach when you listen to patients and colleagues talk about their religious practices.

NURSING ASSESSMENT
OF SPIRITUAL NEEDS

A very practical purpose of a spiritual assessment is to identify ways in which culturally based religious beliefs can affect care, as in the following examples provided by Lipson and Dibble (2005):

- Beliefs about causes of illness (e.g., God's will, supernatural causes, "bad wind," curse of evil spirits, yin/yang, or hot/cold energy imbalance)
- Fasting, abstinence, and selection of foods and fluids (e.g., prohibition of pork, fasting during holy days, fasting during certain illnesses, eating healing foods during certain conditions)
- Acceptability of medical procedures including sterilization, abortion, biopsies, surgery, organ transplants, blood transfusions, and male and female circumcision
- Health-related practices (e.g., immunizations, breastfeeding, postpartum recuperation, protection from sexually transmitted infections)
- Role of healers (e.g., herbalists, faith healers, removal of spells, exorcism of evil spirits)
- Practices that support healing (e.g., prayers, rituals, lighting candles, healing spells, religious promises, use of holy objects)

Two additional purposes of a spiritual assessment are to identify indicators of spiritual distress and to identify ways in which spirituality can be fostered as a health promotion intervention.

The following Wellness Assessment Guide lists questions that can be used to assess spiritual needs.

GUIDE FOR ASSESSING
SPIRITUAL WELLNESS

Ask the following questions about religious and spiritual beliefs and practices:

• Do you consider yourself spiritual or religious?
• Do you belong to any religious groups?
• Are there things we can do while you're here to address
  your spiritual needs (e.g., arrange visits from religious
  support people, provide privacy or resources for spiritual practices)?
• Are there ways in which your religious beliefs need to be
  considered as part of your care (e.g., avoidance or provision of certain types of food, avoidance of treatments
  during prayer times, acceptability of certain medical
  treatments)?
• Do you have spiritual beliefs that help you cope with
  stress or illness?

Ask the following questions to identify spiritual distress:

• Are there ways in which your beliefs are either helpful or
  problematic in relation to your health condition?
• Do you have any concerns about your spiritual
  well-being?
• Are you questioning any of your beliefs because of your
  current situation?
• Do you have any concerns about forgiveness for yourself
  or in your relationships with others?

=== *ESSENTIAL FACTS*

Answers to simple questions asked during routine care activities can provide important assessment information.

Health Promotion in Practice

When you administer medications to Mrs. M, you notice that she seems usually troubled and preoccupied. You take a minute to ask, "How are you feeling in your heart today?" and you find out that she is very worried about her diagnosis and would find comfort in being able to see her minister and ask for prayers from her congregation.

NURSING ACTIONS TO PROMOTE SPIRITUAL WELLNESS

Active Listening and Presence

Nursing actions to promote spiritual wellness are not complicated, and, in fact, can be integral parts of care. Two widely recognized nursing interventions to address spiritual needs are presence and active listening, as described in the following Wellness Activity Tools. These interventions are especially important for patients experiencing spiritual distress because the goal is to facilitate healing by communicating love, empathy, and compassion, even in situations that cannot readily be alleviated.

Wellness Activity Tool: Presence and Active Listening in Nursing Care

Presence is a nursing intervention that involves the conscious act of focusing one's full attention on the patient. Use the following reflective exercise:

- Gather all your attention and call your thoughts and feelings from their wanderings.
- Imagine using a gigantic lasso to pull in all distracting thoughts and feelings.
- Let go of the lasso and watch as all the contents dissipate.
- Now focus on a point in your body such as your heart or the center of your head.
- Use another lasso to gather all your attention to the present moment.
- Pull the lasso in and focus your full attention on your patient.

Use the following everyday nursing routines to promote presence:

- When washing your hands, think about cleansing away all distractions, then focus your attention on your patient as you dry your hands.
- As you pass through the doorway of a patient's room, leave all distractions outside, and focus on the patient as you walk over the threshold.

Active listening is a healing intervention that involves the following communication skills:

- Attending fully to the patient as a whole person
- Listening with all your senses
- Setting aside the need to "fix," "answer," or solve problems
- Being with the patient in silence

- Asking leading questions
- Giving short affirmative responses to encourage self-expression
- Clarifying perceptions and feelings
- Communicating nonjudgmental acceptance
- Expressing empathy and acceptance through your tone of voice
- Using touch and nonverbal communication purposefully
- Taking relaxing breaths and encouraging the patient to do the same

ESSENTIAL FACTS

Enable yourself to be present to patients by clearing your mind of distractions and bringing your attention to your patient while you perform a usual activity.

Wellness in Practice

When you wash your hands, think about cleansing away all distractions with the soap and water, then focus your attention on your patient as you dry your hands.

Responding to Expressions of Spiritual Distress

Communication skills are especially important when patients express indicators of spiritual distress, but this can be quite challenging. Following are some examples of statements that can be adapted for responding to specific aspects of spiritual distress:

- Emotional support: "I'm sure this is a very challenging time for you; what are the sources of strength for you during difficult times like this?"

- Guilt work facilitation: "You've talked about feeling guilty because you could no longer care for your mother in her home. From what you've described, it sounds like you made a very caring decision to make sure that she had the best quality of life for her situation."
- Hope instillation: "It sounds to me like you feel pretty hopeless about being cured. Can you identify any beliefs or people that give you a sense of hope?"
- Lack of acceptance: Verbal and nonverbal indicators of being nonjudgmental and accepting of the patient as a whole person.
- Lack of courage: "I know you said you're afraid that the outcome of surgery will not be good, but you've faced the diagnostic procedures with a lot of courage, and I believe that you'll continue to be courageous even though you may not feel very brave right now."
- Lack of love: "Even though I'm not assigned to care for you today, I want you to know that I was thinking about you and hope for the best when you have surgery tomorrow."
- Feeling abandoned: "I know you said you feel like God has abandoned you, but I believe that if we look in unexpected places, we find clues to His presence. When you've felt like this before, what has helped you find strength?"

ESSENTIAL FACTS

When patients experience spiritual distress or indicate an interest in receiving spiritual care, ask if they would like a referral to a spiritual or religious advisor during the hospitalization or as part of a discharge plan.

Health Promotion in Practice

Mrs. P has been admitted to the hospital twice in the last year for congestive heart failure. She tells you that she feels hopeless about her condition and is especially discouraged because she no longer has the stamina to attend church. You ask if she would like to talk with the pastoral care services, and you initiate a referral for social services to contact the parish nurse program where Mrs. P usually attends church.

Prayer

Prayer is defined as communicating with a spiritual being and is widely accepted as a healing modality. Each individual experiences prayer in a unique way and has many formal and informal expressions, including silence, chanting, singing, dancing, reading, and participating in worship services or prayer with others. Considerations about prayer in clinical settings include:

- Make sure it is voluntary and done only with the patient's permission.
- Ask patients or their visitors about preferences for forms of prayer.
- Arrange for privacy and facilitate an environment in which the patient can pray.

- If the patient desires, arrange for visits by religious support people for shared prayer.
- If you are not comfortable praying with a patient, arrange for other staff or resources to do so.

Encouraging Spiritual Practices for Health Promotion

An important aspect of health promotion is talking with patients about activities that foster spiritual growth and encouraging them to engage in these activities. Many institutional settings provide audiovisual resources for meditation, imagery, prayer, and other spiritual practices, and a relatively simple intervention is to assist patients in accessing these resources. Another way to encourage spiritual practices is to initiate a discussion of activities that promote spiritual wellness such as the following:

- Body–mind practices: prayer, meditation, yoga, tai chi, journaling, guided imagery
- Practices that foster a connection to nature: walking, gardening
- Creative self-expression activities: art, dance, music
- Activities that provide a sense of meaning and purpose: volunteering, caring for others, sharing celebrations and remembrances of life events

SELF-WELLNESS IN PRACTICE

Take a minute now and engage in the reflective exercise in the Wellness Activity Tool on page 73.

ESSENTIAL RESOURCES

American Holistic Nurses Association
ahna.org
George Washington Institute for Spirituality & Health
http://gwish.org
University of Minnesota Center for Spirituality and
Healing
www.csh.edu

7

Overview of Complementary and Alternative Medicine

Complementary and alternative medicine (CAM) is widely used for management of symptoms and prevention of diseases, often as a self-care practice. Nurses are not expected to be experts in CAM, but they are expected to know about commonly used modalities and advise patients in appropriate, safe, and effective use. Nurses may also choose to incorporate complementary and alternative therapies in their patient care or suggest that patients seek additional information about a particular modality. This chapter provides information about complementary and alternative modalities that are pertinent to nursing responsibilities in patient care situations.

In this chapter, you will learn:

1. Definitions and examples of CAM
2. Responsibilities of nurses regarding CAM
3. Safety and efficacy concerns
4. How to talk with patients about CAM
5. Use of CAM in nursing care, including techniques for aromatherapy

WHAT IS CAM?

The National Center on Complementary and Alternative Medicine (NCCAM) defines CAM as a group of diverse medical and health care systems, practices, and products that are not presently part of conventional medicine as practiced by medical doctors, doctors of osteopathy, or their allied health professions, including psychologists, physical therapists, and registered nurses (NCCAM, 2012). Table 7.1 summarizes

TABLE 7.1 Examples of CAM by Category

Type and Description	Examples
Natural products: substances found in nature	Herbs (botanicals), vitamins, minerals, aromatherapy
Mind and body medicine: techniques that enhance the mind's capacity to affect physical functioning and promote health	Yoga, meditation, hypnotherapy, tai chi, qi gong, guided imagery, deep-breathing exercises, acupuncture
Manipulative and body-based practices: therapies based on manipulation or movement of body structures and systems	Massage therapies, spinal manipulation (e.g., chiropractic or osteopathic manipulation)
Movement therapies: movement-based approaches to promote health	Alexander technique, Feldenkrais method, Pilates, Trager Psychophysical Integration, Rolfing Structural Integration
Energy medicine: practices that focus on manipulation of energy fields to affect health	Reiki, acupuncture, Therapeutic Touch, Healing Touch, qi gong, magnet therapy, sound energy therapy, light therapy
Whole medical systems: complete systems of theory and practice that evolved over time in different cultures	Ayurvedic medicine, traditional Chinese medicine, homeopathy, naturopathy

Source: NCCAM (2012).

types and examples of CAM as defined by the NCCAM. Additional clarifications are:

- *Complementary medicine* refers to modalities that are used together with conventional medicine
- *Alternative medicine* refers to modalities that are used in place of conventional medicine
- *Integrative* (or *integrated*) *medicine* refers to a combination of treatments from conventional medicine and CAM

═══ *ESSENTIAL FACTS*

What is considered CAM changes as new evidence emerges and a modality becomes an accepted part of conventional medicine. For example, cognitive-behavioral therapies and patient support groups were initially classified as complementary and alternative modalities.

NURSING RESPONSIBILITIES WITH REGARD TO CAM

Most people use complementary or alternative practices as a self-care practice, and often do so without advice from licensed health care professionals. Patients usually find information from friends, family, self-help books, and media sources, including television and the Internet. It is important to recognize that not all information about CAM is accurate, and this is especially true with regard to products that are promoted for self-care. It is also important to recognize that patients may be reluctant to talk with their primary health care practitioners about complementary and alternative practices they are using or considering. Thus, important nursing responsibilities include the following:

- Addressing safety and efficacy concerns
- Providing a safe environment for patients to talk about CAM
- Facilitating responsible decisions about use of CAM

SAFETY AND EFFICACY CONCERNS

Safety and efficacy concerns about CAM in general center on false advertising; the lack of qualifications for providers; the high cost of care; and the use of unproven remedies, especially in place of proven treatments. In particular, safety concerns related to herbs and other natural products include poor quality of the product, risk of adverse effects and interactions with medications, and inadequate information about ingredients. Based on these concerns, the NCCAM considers most herbal products safe for adults under the following conditions:

- The quality of the product is good and does not contain harmful ingredients.
- The dose is not excessive.
- The product is not used as a substitute for medically necessary drugs.
- The FDA has not issued a safety warning.
- The consumer is aware of possible adverse effects.
- The product is not likely to interact with medications.
- The product is not used before surgery or during the perioperative period.

In addition, the NCCAM advises people who have diabetes and women who are pregnant or nursing to use herbal products only under the direction of their primary care practitioner.

Potential Interactions

It is imperative to consider the possibility of interactions whenever a patient takes an herbal product and a prescription medication. Mechanisms causing herb–drug interactions are similar to those that cause drug–drug interactions: altered absorption, metabolism, or elimination and synergistic, additive, or antagonistic effects. The following Risk Assessment Tool lists examples of herb–drug interactions.

RISK ASSESSMENT TOOL: POTENTIAL HERB–DRUG INTERACTIONS

Herb	Potential Interactions
Black cohosh, chamomile, ginger, kava, St. John's wort, or valerian	Potentiation of drugs that act on the central nervous system (e.g., alcohol, barbiturates, psychoactive drugs)
Evening primrose, feverfew, garlic, ginkgo, American ginseng, saw palmetto, or St. John's wort	Increased risk for bleeding with anticoagulants and nonsteroidal anti-inflammatory drugs
Ginseng	Increased effect of hypoglycemic agents
Green tea	Decreased effectiveness of warfarin
Kava	Decreased effectiveness of drugs for Parkinson's disease
Licorice	Potentiation of oral corticosteroids

St. John's wort	Decreased blood levels of digoxin, statins, theophylline, oral contraceptives, certain antidepressants, and antiretroviral protease inhibitors
Yohimbe	Increased blood pressure with tricyclic antidepressants

TALKING WITH PATIENTS ABOUT CAM

Although most patients who use CAM do not discuss this with their health care practitioners, this is an important component of health promotion for the following reasons:

- To communicate that all health-related interventions affect the overall plan of care
- To identify and document health-related practices and sources of health care used by the patient
- To assess the patient's knowledge about or openness to CAM
- To identify actual or potential adverse effects, such as herb–drug interactions
- To assess health beliefs that influence the choice of interventions and practitioners that the patient will consider using
- To set the stage for teaching patients about making responsible decisions about self-care interventions

NURSING ASSESSMENT

Open-ended questions, when asked nonjudgmentally, are effective for eliciting information about use of CAM. Questions can be asked in relation to prevention or management of a condition that the patient experiences or is concerned about. For example, use a statement such as "People sometimes use relaxation techniques when they are stressed—is there anything that you do when you are dealing with so many demands on your time?" According to a national survey, patients are most likely to use CAM for the following conditions, in order of most frequent use: back pain, neck pain, joint pain, arthritis, anxiety, cholesterol, head or chest cold, other musculoskeletal conditions, severe headache or migraine, and insomnia (Barnes, Bloom, & Nahin, 2008).

The following assessment guide suggests questions that can be used to assess use of CAM.

ASSESSMENT GUIDE FOR USE OF CAM

Ask all patients these or similar questions:

- Do you regularly or periodically use any herbs or other types of products for health purposes?
- Do you engage in any practices that are considered nonmedical or nonconventional to promote health?
- Are you considering using herbs or other therapies for your _____ (e.g., pain, arthritis)?

If a patient is using an herb or other natural product, ask these questions:

- What's the reason you use _____?
- Do you think this has helped you?
- Have you talked with your doctor (nurse practitioner, primary care provider) about [specific product]?
- Have you obtained any information about possible adverse effects associated with [specific product]?
- [If the patient is also taking a prescription drug] Have you checked about any potential herb–drug interactions?

─────────────────────────── *ESSENTIAL FACTS*

It is not necessary to have a lengthy discussion with patients about CAM, but it is important to ask about use of nonprescribed self-care practices.

Health Promotion in Practice

When talking with Ms. P about her back pain, ask, "In addition to taking the medications, is there anything else you do to alleviate your pain?"

TEACHING PATIENTS ABOUT CAM

Nurses have many opportunities to help patients make responsible decisions about CAM by teaching them to use reliable information about specific modalities or products. The NCCAM provides a wealth of evidence-based fact sheets and other up-to-date information for consumers and health care professionals, as do other organizations listed in the ESSENTIAL RESOURCES at the end of this chapter. The following Wellness Activity Tool can be given to patients to advise about safe and effective use of CAM.

Wellness Activity Tool: Safe and Effective Use of CAM

Considerations About Nonprescription or Nonconventional Interventions
• Talk with your primary care practitioner about any therapies you are using or considering using for health-related purposes.
• Recognize that any substance that is ingested, inhaled, or absorbed can have physiologic effects, including adverse effects and interactions.

- Ask your primary care practitioner for advice about nonprescription therapies that may be pertinent to your health.
- When deciding about a CAM modality, find out about its safety and effectiveness, and recognize that testimonials do not constitute evidence of effectiveness.

Considerations About Herbs and Other Natural Products

- Products labeled as "natural" are not necessarily "safe."
- Be aware of adverse effects and herb–drug interactions that can occur.
- Talk with your primary care practitioner about all bioactive substances that you use or are considering using.
- Do not substitute CAM for prescribed therapies without first discussing this with your primary care practitioner.
- Special precautions may be necessary under certain circumstances, including pregnancy, lactation, surgery, and certain medical conditions.
- Be skeptical about information that is based solely on one particular brand.

Considerations for Obtaining Reliable Information About CAM

- Obtain information about CAM from reliable sources, such as the National Center for Complementary and Alternative Medicine, www.nccam.nih.gov.
- Be skeptical about Internet sites that are primarily selling products, which are identified by ".com" in their web address.

- Be aware of key indicators of quackery, such as a sensational writing style, and claims for any of the following: quick, dramatic, or miraculous results; one product cures numerous symptoms; secret ingredients, breakthrough, not available anywhere else.

Considerations for Selecting a CAM Practitioner

- Ask your primary care practitioner for advice about a qualified practitioner.
- Before making an appointment, ask about the practitioner's credentials, experience, training, licenses, or certifications.
- Find out about the cost of treatment and whether any of it is covered by insurance.
- Bring a list of questions to your first visit and evaluate your experience before making another appointment.

USING CAM IN NURSING CARE

Since the time of Florence Nightingale, nurses have used numerous CAM interventions, and nurses are increasingly using a broad range of healing modalities. For example, interventions discussed in this book (in Wellness Activity or Teaching Tools) that nurses can readily incorporate in patient care include prayer, meditation, imagery, affirmations, aromatherapy, and breathing techniques. Organizations listed in the ESSENTIAL RESOURCES can provide information about advanced skills in modalities such as therapeutic touch, healing touch, Reiki, massage, or biofeedback.

ESSENTIAL FACTS

Be aware of safe modalities that can be effective for certain conditions and initiate a discussion about them.

Health Promotion in Practice

When providing care for patients who have fibromyalgia, say, "Many people with fibromyalgia find that guided imagery is helpful in managing their condition. Are you familiar with that or would you be interested in learning about it?"

AROMATHERAPY

Aromatherapy is the use of essential oils for physical, spiritual, and psychological benefits. Nurses in European and other countries have used this as a usual nursing modality for decades, and it is increasingly being incorporated into routine nursing care in the United States. The following Wellness Activity Tool is a guide to using aromatherapy in clinical settings or teaching patients about aromatherapy for self-care.

Wellness Activity Tool: Aromatherapy

Aromatherapy is a safe healing modality that has been used for centuries throughout the world.

Essential Oils
- Are the steam distillates of aromatic plants that are extracted from parts of plants, including flowers, leaves, bark, roots, and seeds

- Are administered through inhalation or topical application
- Can affect all body systems after they reach the circulatory and nervous systems
- Are used for pain relief, relaxation, infections, wound healing, and palliative care

Examples of Therapeutic Uses of Some Essential Oils

- Eucalyptus: Analgesic, antimicrobial, antiseptic, muscle relaxant, insect repellent
- Frankincense: Anti-inflammatory, antimicrobial, sedative, wound healing
- Lavender: Analgesic, antimicrobial, antispasmodic, antiseptic, sedative
- Peppermint: Antimicrobial, anti-inflammatory, antiseptic
- Teatree: Antimicrobial, anti-inflammatory, antiseptic

How to Do

- Inhalation mode: Place 1 to 5 drops of an essential oil on a tissue or use an indirect inhalation method (e.g., burners, nebulizers, vaporizers), then inhale for 5 to 10 minutes.
- Topical application methods: (a) Dilute 4 to 6 drops of essential oil in enough warm water to soak a soft cotton cloth and place it over the affected area for up to 4 hours; (b) Dilute 1 or 2 drops of essential oil in a teaspoon of cold-pressed vegetable oil, cream, or gel, and use as a massage oil.

Considerations

- Obtain essential oils from reputable suppliers.
- Store essential oils in a cool place and away from open flames or sunlight.
- Use cautiously or not at all under certain conditions, including pregnancy, hypertension, seizures, severe asthma, multiple allergies, and estrogen-dependent tumors.
- Test for allergic responses on a small area before applying to a large area.
- Recognize that some essential oils can affect prescription medications, including barbiturates or antibiotics.
- Recognize that essential oils can have adverse effects (e.g., bergamot can cause photosensitivity or skin irritation; mint can cause sleep disturbances).
- Keep oils away from eyes and keep eyes closed during inhalation.
- Essential oils need to be matched correctly with the condition being treated. For example, three different kinds of lavender have different modes of action as (a) a relaxant, (b) a stimulant and expectorant, and (c) an antimicrobial.

SELF-WELLNESS IN PRACTICE

Become more comfortable discussing CAM with patients and considering its use for your health goals by browsing through the information at www.nccam.nih.gov and reading about a modality of interest to you.

ESSENTIAL RESOURCES

Information About CAM

American Holistic Nurses Association
www.ahna.org
Association for Applied Psychophysiology and
Biofeedback
www.aapb.org
Food and Drug Administration
www.fda.gov
Healing Touch Program
www.healingtouch.net
International Association of Reiki Professionals
www.iarp.org
International Center for Reiki Training
www.reiki.org
National Association of Nurse Massage Therapists
www.nanmt.org
National Center for Complementary and Alternative
Medicine
www.nccam.nih.gov
NIH Dietary Supplement Fact Sheet
http://ods.od.nih.gov/factsheets/list-all
Therapeutic Touch International Association
www.therapeutic-touch.org

8

Nutritional Wellness

Good nutrition, adequate physical activity, and stress management are core components of health promotion for wellness for all adults. Good nutrition is an essential intervention for preventing and managing diseases and it is also a major influence on overall health. Thus, a crucial health promotion role for nurses is to teach patients about the importance of choosing foods that nurture their wellness.

In this chapter, you will learn:

1. Ways in which nutrition influences health for adults
2. Cultural and socioeconomic factors that affect nutritional wellness
3. How bioactive substances can affect nutrients
4. How to assess for nutritional wellness
5. Teaching patients about nutrition

RELATIONSHIP OF NUTRITION TO HEALTH

For many decades, health care providers have focused on the role of nutrition in preventing nutritional deficiencies, maintaining basic physiologic functions, and managing diseases. In recent years, this focus has expanded to emphasize the role of nutrition as an intervention for preventing disease and improving overall health. Examples of nutrition as a health promotion intervention are:

- Diets that are rich in fruits and vegetables can reduce the risk of cancer, cardiovascular disease, and other chronic conditions.
- Adequate calcium and vitamin D intake are essential for bone health and prevention of osteoporosis.
- Zinc and copper are important for promoting wound healing.
- Dietary fiber intake plays a role in preventing obesity, diabetes, coronary heart disease, and several types of cancer (Lattimer & Haub, 2010).
- Fruits and vegetables that are high in carotenoids can prevent or delay the development and progression of age-related macular degeneration.
- Adequate fluid intake is important for reducing the risk for urolithiasis, constipation, exercise asthma, and episodes of hyperglycemia in people with diabetes (Manz & Wentz, 2005).
- Foods that are rich in antioxidants, B vitamins, trace minerals, and essential fatty acids can buffer the effects of stress and support overall health and wellness (Luck, 2013).
- High intake of fat, especially animal fat, increases the risk of cancer.

FACTORS THAT CAN AFFECT NUTRITIONAL WELLNESS

Cultural and Socioeconomic Factors

Cultural and socioeconomic factors can affect all the following aspects of nutritional wellness:

- Accessibility to nutritional foods
- Methods of food preparation
- Choice of foods
- Usual times for and frequency of meals
- Usual eating utensils
- Acceptable behaviors related to eating and food preparation
- Meaning and symbolism of certain foods and beverages in daily routines and on special occasions

Low socioeconomic status is a major underlying condition for *food insecurity*, defined as the inability to acquire nutritionally adequate and safe foods to meet one's needs. Since 2008, annual surveys have consistently found that nearly 15% of American households are categorized as food insecure (Coleman-Jensen, Nord, Andrews, & Carlson, 2012). Many studies have identified serious health consequences that are directly linked to food insecurity, including poor glycemic control in diabetics and increased prevalence of obesity, diabetes, and cardiovascular risk factors (Seligman, Jacobs, Lopez, Tschann, & Fernandez, 2012; Seligman, Laraia, & Kushel, 2010). Although resources are available to address food insecurity, many people do not receive benefits for which they are eligible, and only 57% of all food-insecure households participate in federal food and nutrition assistance programmes (Coleman-Jensen et al., 2012). These situations can be addressed by communicating a nonjudgmental attitude, talking about good nutrition as an important health promotion intervention, and providing information about federal and local resources. Also, consider facilitating a referral for social services if the person may be eligible for, but not taking advantage of, federal programmes. In addition to the programmes listed in the ESSENTIAL RESOURCES, many communities and churches sponsor meal programmes or food pantries.

Effects of Bioactive Substances

Bioactive substances—defined as substances that have an effect on living tissue—can affect nutritional wellness by interfering with the absorption or storage of nutrients and by their effects on appetite, food appeal, and digestion. Medications, herbs, dietary supplements, nicotine, and alcohol are examples of bioactive substances that can detrimentally affect nutrients. Table 8.1 provides examples of detrimental effects of some medications on nutrients. Health promotion involves teaching patients how to avoid harmful effects by proactively adjusting nutrient intake, when appropriate, to avoid imbalances.

NURSING ASSESSMENT OF NUTRITIONAL WELLNESS

Nurses assess nutrition not only as an essential component of overall wellness but also in the context of specific health concerns, such as osteoporosis, hypertension, and cardiovascular disease. The following Wellness Assessment Guide can be used to assess a patient's nutritional status and identify learning needs related to promoting nutritional wellness.

TABLE 8.1 Risk Assessment Tool: Effects of Medications on Nutrients

Medication	Effect on Nutrients
Aldactazide or amlodipine	↑ absorption of potassium
Amphotericin B	↑ need for magnesium and potassium
Anticonvulsants	↓ storage of vitamin K, ↓ absorption of calcium
Chlorothiazide, furosemide, gentamicin, or penicillin	↑ excretion of potassium
Colchicine	↓ absorption of fat, protein, iron, calcium, sodium, potassium, carotene, and vitamin A
Corticosteroids	↑ need for calcium and potassium
Laxatives, phenytoin	↓ absorption of fat-soluble vitamins (A, D, E, and K)
Metformin	↓ absorption of vitamin B_{12}
Neomycin	↓ absorption of fat, lactose, calcium, nitrogen, potassium, and vitamin B_{12}
Phenobarbital	↓ absorption of calcium and vitamin D
Sodium bicarbonate	↑ risk of hypernatremia and water retention
Tetracyclines	↓ absorption of zinc, iron, calcium, and magnesium

ASSESSMENT GUIDE FOR NUTRITIONAL WELLNESS

Ask these questions to identify the person's normal patterns:

- What are your usual patterns of eating meals (when, where, with whom, etc.)?
- Describe the type and quantity of food you typically eat.
- Describe the most common ways you prepare meals (e.g., frying, baking, microwaving, steaming).
- Where do you generally obtain your food (e.g., markets, delicatessens, large stores)?

- Do you generally consume fresh, frozen, or canned fruits and vegetables?
- Do you have any difficulties getting groceries or preparing meals?
- Have there been any recent changes in eating or food preparation routines (e.g., change in living arrangements or significant relationships)?

Ask these questions to assess health factors that affect nutrition:

- Do you have any health conditions associated with particular dietary needs (e.g., diabetes, heart disease, liver or kidney failure)?
- Are you aware of any allergies or intolerances to foods or beverages (e.g., lactose intolerance)?
- Have you changed your eating patterns because of health-related concerns (e.g., are there foods you avoid or try to include because of risks for cancer or heart disease)?

Ask questions such as these to explore opportunities for teaching about nutritional wellness:

- Do you have any questions about ways of improving your nutrition?
- Are you interested in learning more about optimal nutrition?

NURSING INTERVENTIONS TO PROMOTE NUTRITIONAL WELLNESS

Nursing interventions to promote nutritional wellness focus on teaching patients about all the following:

- Identify factors that influence their nutrition in both helpful and harmful ways.
- Assess their usual consumption of food and beverages, including types of nutrients and portions of food.

- Compare their usual nutritional intake with the recommendations for their group (e.g., age, level of activity).
- Set specific and realistic short- and long-term goals for improving nutrition.
- Develop a plan for gradually achieving the established goals.

The following sections describe guidelines for teaching about optimal nutrition for adults, and other chapters incorporate information about nutritional interventions pertinent to specific aspects of health promotion. Information about weight management is discussed in Chapter 10. In addition, patients can be encouraged to use interactive tools and other consumer-oriented information available through the organizations listed in the ESSENTIAL RESOURCES section.

Dietary Guidelines for Americans 2010

Every 5 years an external committee appointed by the U.S. Departments of Agriculture and Health and Human Services publishes research-based recommendations about nutritional intake and physical activity levels that are optimal for promoting health and decreasing the risk of nutrition-associated chronic illnesses. Key recommendations identified as most important for improving health are summarized in the following Wellness Teaching Tool (U.S. Department of Agriculture [USDA] & U.S. Department of Health and Human Services [USDHHS], 2010).

Wellness Teaching Tool: Science-Based Advice for Nutrition and Physical Activity

Actions for Balancing Calories to Manage Weight
- Prevent or reduce overweight and obesity through improved eating and physical activity behaviors.
- Control total calorie intake to attain and maintain ideal body weight.
- Increase physical activity and reduce time spent in sedentary behaviors.

- Maintain appropriate caloric balance for each stage of life: childhood, adolescence, adulthood, pregnancy, breastfeeding, and older adulthood.

Foods to Limit or Reduce
- Daily sodium intake of less than 1,500 mg for adults aged 51 and older and those of any age who are African American or have hypertension, diabetes, or chronic kidney disease; daily intake of less than 2,300 mg for all other adults
- Saturated fatty acids: less than 10% of daily calories, replace with monounsaturated and polyunsaturated fatty acids
- Cholesterol: less than 300 mg per day
- Avoid trans fatty acids by limiting foods with partially hydrogenated oils and other sources of synthetic trans fats
- Limit foods containing solid fats, added sugars, refined grains, and sodium
- If alcohol is consumed, limit to one drink daily for women and two daily for men

Foods and Nutrients to Increase
- A variety of fruits and vegetables, especially dark-green, red, and orange vegetables, and beans and peas.
- Consume at least half of grains as whole—rather than refined—grains.
- Increase intake of fat-free or low-fat daily beverages.
- Choose a variety of protein foods, including seafood, lean meat and poultry, eggs, beans and peas, soy products, and unsalted nuts and seeds.
- Choose a variety of seafood in place of some meat and poultry.
- Choose protein foods that are lower in solid fats and calories instead of those that are higher in solid fats.

- Choose the following foods for good sources of potassium, dietary fiber, calcium, and vitamin D: fruits, vegetables, whole grains, milk and milk products.

Recommendations for Specific Groups

- *Women who may become pregnant:* Eat foods that supply heme iron and foods rich in vitamin C and folate; consume 400 mcg per day of synthetic folic acid.
- *Women who are pregnant or breastfeeding:* Take iron supplement as recommended by health care provider; consume 8 to 12 ounces of seafood per week from a variety of sources, except for shark, tilefish, swordfish, and king mackerel, but limit white tuna to 6 ounces per week.
- *People aged 50 years and older:* Consume vitamin B_{12} in fortified cereals or dietary supplements.

FOOD PORTIONS

An important aspect of maintaining optimal nutritional balance is choosing food portions based on recommended serving sizes. It is well known that portion sizes of food have been gradually increasing since the 1970s across all settings (i.e., homes, restaurants, and supermarkets) in the United States. This phenomenon, which is called *portion distortion*, can interfere with weight management and contribute to obesity and other detrimental health consequences. Of particular concern is the significant increase in average portions of foods that are high in fats and sugars. Dietary guidelines differentiate between a *portion*, which is the amount of food a person chooses to eat, and a *serving*, which is the amount of food that is recommended. The serving size card illustrated in Figure 8.1 can be used to teach patients about the amount of food that constitutes a recommended serving. The ESSENTIAL RESOURCES lists good sources of teaching tools, including interactive ones, that provide helpful information related to nutritional wellness.

Cut out and fold on the dotted line. Laminate for longtime use.

1 Serving Looks Like . . .	1 Serving Looks Like . . .
GRAIN PRODUCTS 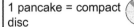	**VEGETABLES AND FRUIT**
1 cup of cereal flakes = fist	1 cup of salad greens = baseball
1 pancake = compact disc 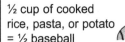	1 baked potato = fist
½ cup of cooked rice, pasta, or potato = ½ baseball	1 med. fruit = baseball
1 slice of bread = cassette tape	½ cup of fresh fruit = ½ baseball
1 piece of cornbread = bar of soap	¼ cup of raisins = large egg

1 Serving Looks Like . . .	1 Serving Looks Like . . .
DAIRY AND CHEESE	**MEAT AND ALTERNATIVES**
1½ oz. cheese = 4 stacked dice or 2 cheese slices	3 oz. meat, fish, and poultry = deck of cards
½ cup of ice cream = ½ baseball	3 oz. grilled/baked fish = checkbook
FATS	
1 tsp. margarine or spreads = 1 dice	2 Tbsp. peanut butter = ping pong ball

FIGURE 8.1 Serving size card.

ESSENTIAL FACTS

One way of promoting self-responsibility for nutritional wellness is by encouraging patients to access reliable consumer-oriented information from sources such as the ones listed in the ESSENTIAL RESOURCES.

SELF-WELLNESS IN PRACTICE

Use the interactive quiz at http://hp2010.nhlbi.net/portion/index.htm to test your knowledge and learn more about changes in portion sizes during the past 2 decades.

ESSENTIAL RESOURCES

American Dietetic Association
www.eatright.org

Food and Nutrition Information Center
National Agricultural Library
www.fnic.nal.usda.gov

Harvard School of Public Health
www.hsph.harvard.edu/nutritionsource

Tufts University, School of Nutrition
http://nutrition.tufts.edu

9

Physical Activity and Musculoskeletal Wellness

Physical activity is a core component of health promotion because it has essential roles in preventing disease and promoting wellness in many ways. Health promotion for musculoskeletal wellness involves all the following aspects:

- *Engaging in adequate physical activity*
- *Moving comfortably, freely, and safely during daily activities*
- *Maintaining optimal strength, flexibility, and endurance for the entire musculoskeletal system*
- *Preventing musculoskeletal discomfort and pathological conditions, such as osteoporosis, fractures, and back pain*

From a health promotion perspective, nurses identify risks that can affect musculoskeletal function, including barriers to physical activity, and teach about interventions.

In this chapter you will learn:

1. Conditions that affect musculoskeletal wellness, including osteoporosis
2. Relationship between physical activity and health promotion
3. Nursing assessment of musculoskeletal wellness
4. Nursing actions to promote musculoskeletal wellness

FACTORS THAT AFFECT MUSCULOSKELETAL WELLNESS

Many conditions affect musculoskeletal wellness, as delineated in Table 9.1 and reviewed in this section. Nurses promote musculoskeletal wellness by teaching patients about actions to prevent or alleviate the negative consequences of these conditions.

TABLE 9.1 Risk Assessment Tool to Identify Conditions That Affect Musculoskeletal Wellness

Condition	Musculoskeletal Effect
Inadequate physical activity	Limitations and discomfort
Inadequate intake of protein, calcium, phosphorus, vitamin D, and zinc	Poor functioning
Occupational activities involving lifting, pushing, pulling, or heavy physical labor	Back pain and disorders affecting the trunk
Frequent engagement in activities involving repetitious movement	Joint disorders such as carpal tunnel syndrome
Risks for falls, slips, or trips (e.g., unsteady gait, sensory impairment, mobility disorders)	Fractures and other serious injuries
Arthritis and other chronic conditions of the musculoskeletal system	Pain, discomfort, limitations affecting daily activities
Osteoporosis	Chronic back pain, increased risk for fractures
Stress-related musculoskeletal tension	Pain and discomfort especially in head, neck, shoulders, and trunk

ESSENTIAL FACTS

An important aspect of health promotion is recognizing that many people experience musculoskeletal tension when they are stressed.

Health Promotion in Practice

Mrs. N reports that she experiences frequent headaches, which are usually accompanied by pain and stiffness in her neck. When you ask further questions, she acknowledges that these episodes occur when her husband is out of town and is unable to assist with care of their three children. This information provides an opportunity to promote wellness by addressing the relationship between stress and headaches.

Osteoporosis

Osteoporosis is an important focus of health promotion for musculoskeletal wellness because serious consequences can be prevented through early detection and the initiation of interventions. Osteoporosis is a condition that commonly affects all older adults as well as adults of any age who have certain risk factors. Most importantly, it is a condition that can be addressed through health promotion interventions. *Primary osteoporosis* affects postmenopausal women and older men and is caused by age-related changes in bone formation that begin in younger adulthood and continue at different rates for men and women. *Secondary osteoporosis*, which can affect adults at any age, is caused by multiple risk factors, including smoking, immobilization, excessive alcohol intake, chronic conditions, and adverse medication effects. The following Risk Assessment Tool lists risks for osteoporosis according to the potential for addressing these conditions. Health promotion interventions are discussed in the section on Nursing Actions.

RISK ASSESSMENT TOOL TO IDENTIFY RISKS FOR OSTEOPOROSIS

Conditions That Respond to Health Promotion Interventions

- Inadequate weight-bearing exercise
- Deficiencies of protein, calcium, vitamin D, and other essential nutrients
- Smoking
- Excessive alcohol use

Conditions That Are Addressed by Primary Care Practitioners

- Endocrine diseases (e.g., hypogonadism, hyper/hypo-thyroidism, insulin-dependent diabetes)
- Hormonal deficiencies due to medical or surgical treatments for diseases, such as prostate or breast cancers
- Certain chronic conditions, including malignancy, rheumatoid disorders, malabsorption syndromes, renal or liver disease
- Long-term use of certain medications (e.g., anticonvulsants, glucocorticoids, immunosuppressive drugs)

Conditions That Cannot Be Changed

- Family history of osteoporosis
- Personal history of fractures
- Women: postmenopausal status (either natural or surgical menopause)
- Men: aged 75 and older

PHYSICAL ACTIVITY

Physical activity—also called exercise—is essential for maintaining musculoskeletal wellness, as well as many other aspects of wellness. Adequate physical activity is mentioned in other chapters of this book as a health promotion intervention, but it is addressed in more detail in this chapter because it is directly dependent on musculoskeletal function. Adequate physical activity promotes wellness by improving all the following aspects of health:

- Musculoskeletal strength and endurance
- Physical stamina
- Posture and appearance
- Prevention and management of osteoporosis
- Cardiovascular health
- Psychological well-being, including improved affect, attitudes, coping skills, and outlook toward life
- Sleep patterns
- Digestive function
- Better body weight
- Stress management

Studies link adequate physical activity to reduced risk of falls, depression, cardiovascular disease, osteoporotic fractures, cognitive decline, type 2 diabetes, and some cancers (e.g., colon, breast, lung, prostate, and endometrial) (Centers for Disease Control and Prevention, 2011b; Conn, Hafdahl, & Mehr, 2011; Ku, Stevinson, & Chen, 2012).

NURSING ASSESSMENT
OF MUSCULOSKELETAL WELLNESS

Nursing assessment to promote musculoskeletal wellness includes all the following:

- Conditions affecting musculoskeletal function and comfort
- Factors that interfere with physical activity
- Identification of limitations that patients may be accepting unnecessarily as inevitable consequences of aging or arthritis
- Risks for long-term consequences, such as fractures, due to osteoporosis

The following Wellness Assessment Guide is useful when assessing overall musculoskeletal function, including patterns of physical activity.

WELLNESS ASSESSMENT GUIDE
FOR MUSCULOSKELETAL FUNCTION

Use the following questions to assess overall musculoskeletal function:

- Do you have any health problems that affect musculoskeletal function or comfort? (If yes, ask pertinent questions about what has been done to have the problem evaluated and treated.)
- Do you experience any difficulties performing daily activities because of limitations or discomfort in any of your joints or muscles?
- Do you avoid certain activities because of limitations or discomfort in any of your joints or muscles?

- Do you chronically or periodically experience pain or discomfort in any joints or muscles?
- Do you have trouble maintaining your balance during usual activities?
- Do you use any supportive devices (e.g., canes, walkers) to move around safely?
- Do you need to hold on to other people to protect you from falling?

Use the following questions to assess usual patterns of physical activity:

- What is your usual pattern of physical activity during a week, including occupational and leisure activities?
- Do you regularly engage in physical activities, such as walking, biking, jogging, swimming, either individually, competitively, or in social groups (e.g., ball games)?
- Do you engage in yoga, tai chi, martial arts, or similar activities?
- What are your goals related to physical activity for health and fitness?
- What interferes with meeting your goals for physical activity (e.g., time constraints, health problems, lack of appropriate equipment or safe and accessible environment)?
- What kind of access do you have to places where you can go for physical activity (e.g., health club, community center, outdoor places that are conducive to biking or walking)?

Incorporate the following observations to assess musculoskeletal function:

- What is the patient's usual height and weight?
- Are there any indicators of gait or balance problems when the patient walks?
- Does the patient have full range of motion in all joints?

- Is the grip strength normal and equal in both hands?
- Are the trunk, hips, and extremities aligned and symmetrical?
- Are there any abnormal curvatures of the spine?
- Can the patient rise from a chair without touching the armrests of the chair or using any other aid?

Finally, for patients who are at risk for osteoporosis, ask whether they have talked with their primary care practitioner about having a bone density test.

ESSENTIAL FACTS

Nurses have many opportunities to assess overall musculoskeletal function by observing patients during the course of usual care.

Health Promotion in Practice

While you are accompanying Ms. C to the bathroom from her bed, you note that she has a very unsteady gait and would be at risk for falls if she did not have assistance. When you ask about this, she reports that she "favors" her left knee and hip due to arthritis, which she has self-diagnosed but has never had evaluated. You advise her to talk to her primary care practitioner for evaluation and consider a referral for physical therapy.

NURSING INTERVENTIONS TO PROMOTE MUSCULOSKELETAL WELLNESS

Teaching Patients About Health Promotion for Musculoskeletal Wellness

Teaching patients about self-care actions for musculoskeletal wellness focuses on promoting adequate physical activity and preventing osteoporosis and fractures, as summarized in this Wellness Teaching Tool.

Wellness Teaching Tool for Promoting Musculoskeletal Wellness

Self-Care Actions to Promote Musculoskeletal Wellness

- Engage in moderately intense physical activity, such as walking briskly, bicycling, dancing, or mowing the lawn, for 30 minutes or more at least 5 days a week.
- Ensure an adequate intake of the following nutrients: calcium, vitamin D, phosphorus, protein, and zinc.
- Be aware of muscle tension; then intentionally relax any tight muscles.
- Pay attention to body position, especially when sitting, standing, or moving, and ensure proper alignment, optimal support, and good balance.
- Engage in activities, such as yoga or tai chi, that contribute to body–mind wellness.
- When engaging in activities that can cause injury, use appropriate safety gear such as a helmet, shin guards, and joint protectors.

To Prevent Osteoporosis and Fractures

- Do not smoke.
- Do not drink excessive amounts of alcohol.
- If you have any risk factors for osteoporosis, including being aged 65 or older, talk with your primary care practitioner about detecting and monitoring any loss of bone mass.
- Talk with your primary care practitioner about the need for calcium and vitamin D supplements.

- Engage in weight-bearing exercise (i.e., physical activity that requires you to be in an upright position).
- Engage in yoga, tai chi, or other activities to improve overall balance and musculoskeletal strength and flexibility.
- Take precautions to protect from falls.

=== *ESSENTIAL FACTS*

Help patients identify simple self-care actions to release physical tension due to stress.

Health Promotion in Practice

Ms. N recognizes that when she is stressed, the right side of her neck feels tight and painful. You suggest that when she experiences this, she takes a deep breath in and then exhales while gently moving her head in a full circle. She also might apply self-massage techniques to address specific areas of muscle tension.

Promoting Adequate Physical Activity

Helping patients overcome barriers to physical activity is another nursing action to promote musculoskeletal wellness. The following Wellness Activity Tool is useful as a guide to address conditions that interfere with obtaining adequate physical activity.

Wellness Activity Tool: Tips for Overcoming Barriers to Physical Activity

Barrier	Try This
Lack of time	• Incorporate physical activity during usual activities, such as exercising while you watch television, parking further away from your destination, using steps instead of elevators or escalators, and walking while you converse on a cell or battery-operated phone
	• Identify three 30-minute periods a week during which you could replace a sedentary activity with a physical activity
Stress	• Use physical activity to relieve stress, even if this involves pacing around your house instead of sitting and fretting
Lack of motivation	• Make a list of all the ways in which you can benefit from exercise and post this in a place where you will review it frequently
	• Set goals and make a plan that is realistic; reward yourself when you reach "achievement points"

- Ask someone whom you care about (e.g., spouse, family, friend) to engage in physical activity with you on a regular schedule (e.g., once or twice weekly) and make a commitment to this plan
- Participate in group sports or recreational activities that involve physical activity (e.g., bowling, kayaking, biking, skating, ball games, line dancing)
- Develop interests that can be productive, enjoyable, and health enhancing (e.g., gardening, yard work, pushing a stroller, walking a dog, playing outdoors with children, or washing windows or floors)

Lack of energy
- Schedule physical activity for times in the day or week when you feel more energetic
- Convince yourself that if you give it a chance, physical activity will increase your energy level—then, try it

Lack of skill or resources
- Choose familiar activities that require little or no equipment (e.g., walking, jogging, or climbing stairs)

	• Find a friend who is willing to help you develop skills
	• Enroll in a class at a community center
	• Recognize that it is important to begin any new activity slowly and work your way toward increased skill and endurance
Fear of injury	• Warm up before and cool down after any strenuous physical activity
	• Wear supportive and comfortable footwear that is most appropriate for the activity
	• Use appropriate safety and protective gear (helmet, joint protectors, shin guards)
	• Choose activities that involve minimal risk

SELF-WELLNESS IN PRACTICE

Begin using a step counter (pedometer) to assess your current level of physical activity; if your level is below 10,000 steps a day, develop a plan to gradually increase your activity level.

ESSENTIAL RESOURCES

Many organizations provide educational materials about osteoporosis, physical activity, and other topics pertinent to health promotion for musculoskeletal wellness. Some materials are available in Spanish and other languages, and many of these materials are free.

America on the Move Foundation
https://aom3.americaonthemove.org

American Cancer Society
www/cancer.org

American Heart Association
www.heart.org

Arthritis Foundation
www.arthritis.org

National Institute of Arthritis and Musculoskeletal and Skin Diseases
www.niams.nih.gov

National Cancer Institute
www.cancer.gov

National Osteoporosis Foundation
www.nof.org

Nursing Actions for Specific Aspects of Health Promotion

10

Weight Management and Digestive Wellness

Physiologically, digestion is a relatively straightforward process that involves the consumption of food and beverages, the absorption of useful nutrients, and the elimination of waste products. From a broader health promotion perspective, however, digestive wellness, including weight management, is affected by many interacting physical, cognitive, emotional, cultural, and socioeconomic factors.

In this chapter, you will learn:

1. Factors that affect digestive wellness
2. How to assess digestive wellness
3. Teaching patients to promote digestive wellness
4. Talking with patients about weight management
5. Health promotion interventions related to colorectal cancer

FACTORS THAT AFFECT DIGESTIVE WELLNESS

Digestive wellness is influenced by many interacting conditions, such as:

- Circulation of blood and lymph for absorption of nutrients
- Elimination of waste products through the intestines, skin, lungs, kidneys, and sweat glands
- Autonomic nervous system control over gastrointestinal activity
- Intestinal secretion of gastrin and secretin hormones that affect the release of substances directly involved with digestion
- Intestinal secretion of ghrelin, leptin, cholecystokinin, and gastric-inhibitory peptide, which are hormones that send signals to the brain and affect appetite and perception of fullness
- Characteristics of the food items, including smell and taste sensations
- Condition of the mouth, teeth, and related structures
- Physical, cognitive, emotional, environmental, and sociocultural factors that influence eating patterns
- Functional abilities related to obtaining, preparing, and consuming food

Table 10.1 lists examples of conditions that affect eating patterns and digestion.

TABLE 10.1 Risk Assessment Tool: Conditions That Affect Eating Patterns and Digestion	
Condition	**Effect on Eating and Digestion**
Teeth missing or in poor condition, gum disease, oral problems, difficulty with chewing or swallowing	Limited types of food intake

(continued)

TABLE 10.1 (continued)

Functional limitations with cognition, vision, mobility, fine-motor movement, or other abilities	Difficulty with obtaining food and preparing meals
Depression, dementia, other conditions affecting mental health	Poor appetite, eating disorders
Lactose intolerance	Digestive problems such as diarrhea, excessive gas, or abdominal cramping after ingestion of milk products
Gluten intolerance	Poor absorption of fats and carbohydrates, causing digestive problems such as bloating, abdominal distension, and stools that are loose, bulky, and greasy
Food allergies	Limited or restricted food choices
Inadequate fiber, adverse medication effects, pathologic conditions that slow peristalsis or affect muscle contractions	Constipation
Stress	Changes in eating patterns, altered bowel movements

ESSENTIAL FACTS

Keep in mind that stress and anxiety exert a wide range of effects on digestive wellness.

Health Promotion in Practice

Mrs. F states that she has been "binge eating for a couple of months ever since my husband lost his job." You help her explore healthier coping behaviors, and talk with her about the relationship between stress and health.

Effects of Bioactive Substances

Bioactive substances that can affect eating patterns and digestive processes include alcohol, caffeine, herbal products, and medications (including illicit, prescription, and over-the-counter ones). These effects can be therapeutic and intentional or they can be adverse and unintentional, as in the examples listed in Table 10.2. It is beyond the scope of this text to cite all effects of bioactive substances on digestive function; however, it is important to assess for common adverse effects of medications and other bioactive substances that affect eating and digestion. For example, gastrointestinal disturbances are common side effects of many herbs. In addition, consider the effects of bioactive substances on nutrients, as discussed in Chapter 8.

TABLE 10.2 Risk Assessment Tool: Effects of Medications on Digestive Wellness

Medication Examples	Effect on Digestion
Narcotics, anticholinergics, iron, aluminum- or calcium-containing products	Slowed gastrointestinal function, constipation
Antihistamines, chemotherapy agents, bronchodilators	Anorexia, weight loss from poor appetite
Aluminum- or magnesium-based products	Stimulation of the gastrointestinal tract, diarrhea
Nonsteroidal anti-inflammatory agents, including aspirin	Gastric irritation, ↑ risk of ulcers and gastrointestinal bleeding
Bulk-forming agents	Early satiety
Anticholinergic or potassium-depleting effects	↑ risk of paralytic ileus

OVERWEIGHT AND OBESITY

Weight management is the most common health concern associated with digestive wellness, as indicated by the fact that

68% of adults in the United States meet criteria for being overweight or obese, and one third of these are obese (National Institute of Diabetes, Digestion, and Kidney Disease [NIDKK], 2010). Moreover, the prevalence of obesity in the United States and worldwide has been increasing steadily in recent decades and is now at epidemic/pandemic proportions (Cornier, Marshall, Hill, Maahs, & Eckel, 2011). It is widely recognized not only as a chief preventable cause of death, disease, and disability but also as a condition that contributes to significant increases in health care costs. In addition to being a major risk factor for type 2 diabetes and coronary heart disease, overweight and obesity increase the risk of stroke, hypertension, osteoarthritis, dyslipidemia, gallbladder disease, menstrual irregularities, complications of pregnancy, gastroesophageal reflux disease, nonalcoholic fatty liver disease, sleep apnea and other breathing problems, and some forms of cancer (e.g., breast, colorectal, endometrial, and kidney).

The "epidemic" of obesity in the United States is a major focus of health promotion as a multifaceted health issue with contributing and interacting factors that include genetic, environmental, behavioral, social, cultural, economic, and emotional components. Physiologically, weight gain occurs when caloric intake consistently exceeds energy needs; however, people vary considerably in their ability to efficiently use nutrients, expend energy, and store and mobilize fat. The simple—and universally applicable—mathematics of weight loss is that an individual needs to expend more calories in physical activity than he or she consumes in food.

ESSENTIAL FACTS

Recognize that two thirds of Americans are overweight or obese according to body mass index (BMI) criteria and that this puts them at increased risk for health problems, even if they don't experience weight-related problems currently.

RISKS FOR COLORECTAL CANCER

Colorectal cancer is one of the most preventable types of cancer and is also one of the most curable types, as long as it is diagnosed early and precancerous growths are removed. Factors that increase the risk for developing colorectal cancer include:

- Being aged 50 years and over, with the risk doubling during each succeeding decade
- Presence or history of colorectal polyps
- History of breast, uterine, ovarian, or colorectal cancer
- History of inflammatory bowel disease
- Personal or family history of colorectal cancer or polyps
- Smoking
- Diet high in fat, red meat, or processed meat
- Obesity
- Physical inactivity
- Excessive alcohol
- Racial or ethnic groups: African American, Ashkenazi Jews

NURSING ASSESSMENT OF DIGESTIVE WELLNESS

From a health promotion perspective, assessment of digestive wellness includes questions about physiologic aspects of the entire gastrointestinal tract and about the many factors that affect eating patterns. Assessment of BMI, illustrated in Figure 10.1, and waist circumference measures are important for identifying overweight and obesity as a health hazard that needs to be addressed. When assessing patients who are aged 50 or older, incorporate a question about colorectal cancer to set the stage for teaching about this. The Assessment Guide for Nutritional Wellness (Chapter 8) can be used in conjunction with the following assessment tool for assessing overall gastrointestinal function, including oral factors that affect eating.

BMI	19	20	21	22	23	24	25	26	27	28	29	30	31	32	33	34	35	36
Height (inches)	Body Weight (pounds)																	
58	91	96	100	105	110	115	119	124	129	134	138	143	148	153	158	162	167	172
59	94	99	104	109	114	119	124	128	133	138	143	148	153	158	163	168	173	178
60	97	102	107	112	118	123	128	133	138	143	148	153	158	163	168	174	179	184
61	100	106	111	116	122	127	132	137	143	148	153	158	164	169	174	180	185	190
62	104	109	115	120	126	131	136	142	147	153	158	164	169	175	180	186	191	196
63	107	113	118	124	130	135	141	146	152	158	163	169	174	180	186	191	197	203
64	110	116	122	128	134	140	145	151	157	163	169	174	180	186	192	197	204	209
65	114	120	126	132	138	144	150	156	162	168	174	180	186	192	198	204	210	216
66	118	124	130	136	142	148	155	161	167	173	179	186	192	198	204	210	216	223
67	121	127	134	140	146	153	159	166	172	178	185	191	198	204	211	217	223	230
68	125	131	138	144	151	158	164	171	177	184	190	197	203	210	216	223	230	236
69	128	135	142	149	155	162	169	176	182	189	196	203	209	216	223	230	236	243
70	132	139	146	153	160	167	174	181	188	195	202	209	216	222	229	236	243	250
71	136	143	150	157	165	172	179	186	193	200	208	215	222	229	236	243	250	257
72	140	147	154	162	169	177	184	191	199	206	213	221	228	235	242	250	258	265
73	144	151	159	166	174	182	189	197	204	212	219	227	235	242	250	257	265	272
74	148	155	163	171	179	186	194	202	210	218	225	233	241	249	256	264	272	280
75	152	160	168	176	184	192	200	208	216	224	232	240	248	256	264	272	279	287
76	156	164	172	180	189	197	205	213	221	230	238	246	254	263	271	279	287	295
BMI	37	38	39	40	41	42	43	44	45	46	47	48	49	50	51	52	53	54

FIGURE 10.1 Body mass index (BMI) calculator.

(continued)

	177	181	186	191	196	201	205	210	215	220	224	229	234	239	244	248	253	258
58	177	181	186	191	196	201	205	210	215	220	224	229	234	239	244	248	253	258
59	183	188	193	198	203	208	212	217	222	227	232	237	242	247	252	257	262	267
60	189	194	199	204	209	215	220	225	230	235	240	245	250	255	261	266	271	276
61	195	201	206	211	217	222	227	232	238	243	248	254	259	264	269	275	280	285
62	202	207	213	218	224	229	235	240	246	251	256	262	267	273	278	284	289	295
63	208	214	220	225	231	237	242	248	254	259	265	270	278	282	287	293	299	304
64	215	221	227	232	238	244	250	256	262	267	273	279	285	291	296	302	308	314
65	222	228	234	240	246	252	258	265	270	276	282	288	294	300	306	312	318	324
66	229	235	241	247	253	260	266	272	278	284	291	297	303	309	315	322	328	334
67	236	242	249	255	261	268	274	280	287	293	299	306	312	319	325	331	338	344
68	243	249	256	262	269	276	282	289	295	302	308	315	322	328	335	341	348	354
69	250	257	263	270	277	284	291	297	304	311	318	324	331	338	345	351	358	365
70	257	264	271	278	285	292	299	306	313	320	327	334	341	348	255	262	369	376
71	265	272	279	286	293	301	308	315	322	329	338	343	351	358	365	372	379	386
72	272	279	287	294	302	309	316	324	331	338	346	353	364	368	375	383	390	397
73	280	288	295	302	310	318	325	333	340	348	355	363	371	378	386	393	401	408
74	287	295	303	311	319	326	334	342	350	358	365	373	381	389	396	404	412	420
75	295	303	311	319	327	335	343	351	359	367	375	383	391	399	407	715	423	431
76	304	312	320	328	336	344	353	361	369	377	385	394	402	410	418	426	435	443

FIGURE 10.1 Body mass index (BMI) calculator (continued).

Source: National Heart Lung and Blood Institute, http://nhlbisupport.com/bmi

NURSING ASSESSMENT OF GASTROINTESTINAL FUNCTION

Assessing Oral Factors That Affect Eating

- Do you have your natural teeth or partial or full dentures?
- Do you have any toothaches or other trouble with your teeth?
- Do you have any soreness or bleeding in your gums or mouth?
- Do you have problems with dry mouth or tongue?
- Do you have any trouble with chewing, or are there foods you avoid because of difficulty with chewing or swallowing?
- How often do you brush and floss your teeth?
- How often do you see the dentist and when was your last dental appointment?
- (If the patient does not go at least once a year, or has not gone in more than a year) What prevents you from going to the dentist for regular check-ups?

Assessing Patterns of Bowel Elimination

- How often do you have a bowel movement?
- Have you noticed any changes in your pattern of bowel movements?
- Do you have any difficulty with bowel movements (e.g., constipation, diarrhea, straining)?
- Do you have episodes of losing control over your bowels?
- Do you take laxatives or any other product to help with constipation?
- Do you have any pain or bleeding when you move your bowels?

Assessing Knowledge About Colorectal Cancer (for Patients Who Are Aged 50 Years and Older)
• Have you had, or talked with your primary care practitioner about, any tests for early detection of polyps or colorectal cancer?

NURSING INTERVENTIONS TO PROMOTE DIGESTIVE WELLNESS

Health promotion for digestive wellness focuses on teaching patients about health practices that affect digestion, interventions to attain and maintain optimal weight, and preventive measures related to colorectal cancer. The following Wellness Teaching Tool summarizes key points to cover when teaching patients about practices to promote digestive wellness.

Wellness Teaching Tool: Actions to Promote Digestive Wellness

Overall Health Practices
• Choose foods and beverages that support your health.
• Follow safety guidelines for obtaining, storing, preparing, and cooking all food items to protect from food-borne illnesses.
• Use relaxation methods when feeling stressed.

Steps to Maintain Good Bowel Habits
• Consume at least 25 g of fiber daily, drink plenty of water, and avoid eating refined foods.
• Engage in daily physical activity.
• Respond quickly to the urge for a bowel movement.
• Avoid using enemas or laxatives.

• Periodically observe bowel movements so you know what's normal and talk with your primary care practitioner if you notice any changes.

Actions for Good Oral Care
• Brush teeth and tongue after meals.
• Floss teeth daily.
• Have teeth cleaned and checked at least annually.
• Maintain good hydration and consume foods high in calcium and phosphorus.

ESSENTIAL FACTS

Address oral health as an integral aspect of promoting digestive wellness.

Health Promotion in Practice

You note that Mr. T's teeth are stained and there is observable tartar around his teeth, and you know that his financial assets are limited. You inform him that the dental school at the local university provides low-cost dental evaluations and care.

Teaching About Weight Management

Achieving and maintaining optimal weight—defined as BMI between 18.5 and 24.9—is a health promotion goal for at least two thirds of adults. This is challenging because despite the proliferation of information touting products that are "guaranteed" effective for weight loss, there is no scientifically sound, quick, and easy solution to weight management. In fact, the consensus among health care professionals is that a multifaceted approach needs to include physical activity, dietary monitoring and modifications, and interventions to address stress and psychological and behavioral factors. If these interventions are not effective, or when the patient needs to lose a significant amount of weight, then pharmacologic or surgical interventions may be appropriate. Wellness Teaching Tools in Chapter 8 can be used to teach about healthy nutrition, particularly with regard to healthy serving size.

The National Institutes of Health (2007) urges health care professionals to initiate brief conversations with patients about weight management and to base these discussions on behavior-change models that have been used successfully for promoting tobacco cessation and increased physical activity. The following Wellness Teaching Tool, which is based on recommendations of the National Institutes of Health (2007), can be used as a guide to discussing weight management with patients.

Wellness Teaching Tool: Talking With Patients About Weight Loss

Initiating the Conversation
- Use preferred terms: "weight" or "excess weight."
- Terms to avoid: "obesity" or "fat."
- Approach the topic for patients who have a BMI of 30 or above.
- Approach the topic for patients who have a weight-related health issue and a BMI between 25 and 29.9 or a waist measurement of over 35 (women) or 40 (men) inches.
- Be aware of and show respect for cultural influences.

Assessing Patient Readiness
- Inquire about patient goals for weight management.
- Ask, "What changes are you ready to make with regard to eating and physical activity?"
- Ask, "What would help you achieve your goals?"

Assist With Setting a Weight Goal
- A sensible 6-month goal is a 5% to 10% reduction.
- A safe and reasonable short-term goal is ½ to 2 pounds per week.
- Preventing weight gain is an appropriate goal for some.

Teach About Healthy Eating and Regular Physical Activity
- Eat a variety of nutritious foods and limit intake of saturated and trans fats, added sugars, salt, and alcohol.
- To maintain weight and promote health: Be physically active for at least 30 minutes on most or all days; set goals for moderate-intensity physical activities, and gradually increase activity level.
- To lose weight or sustain weight loss: Be physically active for 60 to 90 minutes a day.
- Incorporate simple activities into daily routines: Use stairs instead of elevators, park farther from entrances, engage in enjoyable physical activities rather than sedentary ones.
- Write down every food item you eat and review this to identify ways of improving eating habits.
- Pay attention to serving size, use smaller amounts of high-calorie foods and larger amounts of fruits and vegetables.
- At restaurants, eat only half the meal and take the rest home.

ESSENTIAL FACTS

Referring to "weight management" as an "act of health" is a positive and nonjudgmental way to start a conversation about this topic with patients.

Teaching About Colorectal Cancer

Teaching about colorectal cancer is an important aspect of health promotion for patients who are aged 50 years and older for the following reasons, cited by Ueland, Hornung, and Greenwald (2006):

- Physical activity and dietary practices can prevent up to 70% of the cases.
- Early detection is associated with a cure rate of more than 90%.
- Screening for colorectal cancer is underutilized.
- Fewer than 40% of cases are diagnosed at the most treatable stage.

Screening for colorectal cancer involves annual fecal occult blood or fecal immunochemical tests in combination with flexible sigmoidoscopy or double-contrast barium enema. A major responsibility of nurses is to encourage patients to talk with their primary care practitioners about screening at appropriate intervals.

SELF-WELLNESS IN PRACTICE

Use Figure 10.1 or the interactive tool at nhlbisupport.com to calculate your BMI and identify appropriate weight management goals. If you are among the one third of Americans with a BMI less than 25, recognize the importance of maintaining your healthy weight.

ESSENTIAL RESOURCES

American Cancer Society
www.cancer.org

Prevent Cancer
http://preventcancer.org

Weight Control Information (WIN), National Institute of Diabetes and Digestive and Kidney Diseases
http://win.niddk.nih.gov

National Heart Lung and Blood Institute (National Institutes of Health)
www.nhlbi.nih.gov

II

Cardiovascular Wellness

Cardiovascular wellness is an essential topic for health promotion for adults because heart disease accounts for one out of every three deaths reported each year in the United States. Additional reasons for the importance of this topic are that at least half of the adult population in the United States has one or more risk factors and that the majority of risks can be reduced through health-promoting actions. Thus, this chapter focuses on helping patients reduce the risk of cardiovascular disease.

In this chapter, you will learn:

1. Risks for cardiovascular disease
2. Nursing assessment of cardiovascular wellness
3. Teaching patients to promote cardiovascular wellness

RISKS FOR CARDIOVASCULAR DISEASE

Cardiovascular wellness is affected by all the following factors that are within the realm of health promotion: smoking, diet, level of physical activity, body mass index (BMI), blood pressure, lipid and triglyceride levels, stress, and exposure to secondhand smoke, as summarized in the Risk Assessment Tool. Other factors that increase the risk of cardiovascular disease—but are not within the scope of primary prevention—include heredity, increased age, pathological conditions, and occupational and socioeconomic influences. Conditions that are addressed by primary care practitioners as risk factors for cardiovascular disease include sleep apnea, menopausal hormone therapy, birth control pills, and calcium supplementation for osteoporosis.

Tobacco in any form is a major avoidable risk for cardiovascular disease. Examples of detrimental effects of nicotine, which are in addition to and independent of the increased risk for many types of cancer, are:

- Acceleration of atherosclerotic process
- Increased blood pressure
- Compromised functioning of cilia in the lungs
- Increased level of low-density lipoprotein (LDL, or "bad" cholesterol)
- Decreased level of high-density lipoprotein (HDL, or "good" cholesterol)

Information about helping patients quit smoking is discussed in Chapter 12, and is applicable to prevention of cardiovascular disease.

RISK ASSESSMENT TOOL: CONDITIONS THAT INCREASE THE RISK OF HEART DISEASE

- Chewing or smoking tobacco in any form
- Exposure to secondhand smoke
- Waist circumference greater than 40 inches in men or 35 inches in women
- Body mass index greater than 25
- Blood pressure greater than 120/80 mmHg
- Total cholesterol higher than 200 mg/dL
- LDL cholesterol higher than 129 mg/dL (borderline high) or 160 mg/dL (optimal is 100 mg/dL or lower)
- HDL cholesterol less than 40 mg/dL (optimal is 60 mg/dL or higher)
- Triglycerides of 150 mg/dL or higher
- Fasting glucose level greater than 100
- High levels of stress

ESSENTIAL FACTS

Stress and anxiety play an important, but often hidden, role in heart disease.

Health Promotion in Practice

Mr. M has several risk factors for cardiovascular disease, and he tells you that he feels much more stressed whenever he has tried to stop smoking, so he justifies smoking as "the lesser of two evils." You suggest to him that the American Heart Association has useful information, including tips on handling the stress of not smoking.

NURSING ASSESSMENT OF CARDIOVASCULAR WELLNESS

Nursing assessment to promote cardiovascular wellness focuses on risks for cardiovascular disease and identification of symptoms of heart disease that require further evaluation, as summarized in the following Assessment Guide.

ASSESSMENT GUIDE FOR CARDIOVASCULAR WELLNESS

Use these questions to identify conditions that can affect cardiovascular wellness:

- Do you ever experience chest pain or other symptoms that may be indicators of heart problems?
- Do you have diabetes, high blood pressure, peripheral vascular disease, or problems with cholesterol or triglycerides?
- Do you smoke?
- Do your parents or siblings have heart disease?
- Do you have sleep apnea?
- Do you work or live in an environment where you are exposed to smoke?

Ask about the following behaviors that affect cardiovascular wellness:

- What is your usual level of physical activity?
- What is your usual dietary intake for a day?
- What methods do you use to reduce stress in daily life?

Incorporate information about all the conditions listed in the Risk Assessment Tool.

====================== *ESSENTIAL FACTS*

Promote self-responsibility for health by encouraging patients to use an interactive Risk Assessment Tool such as the one at http://millionhearts.hhs.gov/resources/tools.html to identify their risk of heart attack or dying from coronary heart disease.

NURSING INTERVENTIONS TO PROMOTE CARDIOVASCULAR WELLNESS

Teaching about actions to promote cardiovascular wellness is multifaceted and encompasses all the following aspects, which are discussed in other chapters: Stress, diet, physical activity, weight management, and smoking are conditions that are most amenable to health promotion interventions, as discussed in Chapters 5, 8, 9, 10, and 12, respectively. The following Wellness Teaching Tool summarizes actions patients can take to promote cardiovascular wellness. In addition, patients can be taught about the recommendations of the U.S. Preventive Services Task Force that daily aspirin can be helpful for preventing cardiovascular disease under certain conditions, as discussed in Chapter 4. The ESSENTIAL RESOURCES lists organizations that provide useful educational materials pertinent to cardiovascular wellness.

Wellness Teaching Tool for Promoting Cardiovascular Wellness

Self-Care Actions to Promote Cardiovascular Wellness
• Do not smoke.
• Engage in moderate physical activity for 30 minutes at least 5 days a week.

- Maintain weight within normal limits.
- Avoid breathing secondary smoke and other air pollutants whenever possible.
- Engage in stress management activities such as meditation and yoga.
- Eat heart-healthy foods, as described in the next section.

Heart-Healthy Eating Patterns

- Consume at least 3 to 5 servings of fruits daily, especially the deeply colored ones.
- Consume at least 3 to 5 servings of vegetables daily, especially the deeply colored ones.
- Include 2 to 3 servings of low-fat or nonfat dairy products.
- Choose whole-grain products as sources of carbohydrates and fiber (e.g., rye, barley, oats, whole wheat).
- Aim for at least 25 g of fiber daily.
- Choose only the leanest meats, poultry, fish, and shellfish.
- Avoid foods that are high in calories, trans fats, or refined sugars.
- Use oils that are least saturated (e.g., canola, safflower, sunflower, corn, olive, soybean, and peanut oils; use margarine that is soft and free of trans fats).
- Limit salt intake to no more than 1,500 mg daily.

ESSENTIAL FACTS

Be aware of opportunities to teach patients about quick-and-easy relaxation methods, such as deep breathing, as methods of managing stress and promoting cardiovascular wellness.

SELF-WELLNESS IN PRACTICE

Take time for a self-assessment by using the interactive tool My Life Check at http://millionhearts.hhs.gov/resources/tools.html to identify ways of promoting cardiovascular wellness for yourself.

ESSENTIAL RESOURCES

American Heart Association
www.americanheart.org

DASH Diet Eating Plan
http://dashdiet.org

Go Red for Women
www.goredforwomen.org

Million Hearts Initiative
http://millionhearts.hhs.gov

National Heart Lung and Blood Institute
www.nhlbi.nih.gov

Women's Heart Foundation
www.womensheart.org

12

Respiratory Wellness

Breathing is essential to all life, yet it is often overlooked as a focus of health promotion. Health promotion for respiratory wellness focuses on all the following aspects:

- *Tobacco smoking: not starting, quitting, avoiding secondhand smoke, supporting smoking cessation for others*
- *Methods of using breathing for relaxation and stress reduction*
- *Prevention of respiratory infections and other conditions that affect breathing*

In this chapter, you will learn:

1. Conditions that affect respiratory wellness
2. Nursing assessment of respiratory wellness
3. Nursing actions to promote overall respiratory health
4. Guidelines for helping smokers quit smoking

FACTORS THAT AFFECT RESPIRATORY WELLNESS

Without even a conscious effort, healthy adults breathe about 20,000 times a day. Each breath is one component of the complex process of respiration that involves intake and movement of air in and out of the lungs, diffusion of gases between the alveoli and the blood, and transport of oxygen to and carbon dioxide from all cells in the body. Because every physiologic function depends on the respiratory function to supply oxygen and to remove carbon dioxide, breathing is often considered tantamount to one's life force. In addition to smoking and pathologic conditions, all the following factors directly affect respiratory function:

- Patency of passageways from the nose and mouth to the alveoli and capillaries
- Movement and flexibility of the diaphragm, chest wall, and all accessory muscles
- Functioning of the cardiovascular system
- Status of all peripheral tissues where gas exchange takes place
- Signals from the central and autonomic nervous systems
- Body posture and position
- Quantity and quality of air in the environment, including secondhand smoke

An important part of health promotion for respiratory wellness is identifying the many interacting factors that affect respiratory function, as delineated in Table 12.1.

SMOKING

Tobacco use is widely recognized as the leading preventable cause of disease, disability, and death in the United States, accounting for one third of all cancers. Smoking directly affects

TABLE 12.1 Risk Assessment Tool to Identify Conditions That Affect Respiratory Wellness

Condition	Effect on Respiratory Function
Smoking	Severely compromised respiratory function, increased incidence of many diseases
Exposure to secondhand smoke	Greater risk for developing cancer, heart disease, and many other diseases
Exposure to respiratory toxins and irritants, such as smoke, pollen, and pollutants	Chronic lung diseases, bronchitis, asthma, emphysema, allergic reactions
Occupational exposure to toxins such as silica, asbestos, coal dust, or agent orange	Increased risk for developing respiratory disease, even after retirement or changing jobs
Poor posture, scoliosis, kyphosis, bed rest	Diminished lung expansion
Sedentary lifestyle	Compromised respiratory function due to deconditioning
Obesity	Limited lung expansion
Sleep apnea	Periods of anoxia during sleep
Medical conditions that affect cardiac or respiratory function; postanesthesia effects	Compromised respiratory function
Medications that depress the respiratory center (narcotics, some antipsychotics)	Compromised respiratory function
Anxiety, fear	Shallow and rapid breathing

respiratory function and increases the risk of all the following serious conditions:

- Cardiovascular disease
- Many types of cancers
- Cataracts, macular degeneration
- Osteoporosis

- Hearing impairment
- Erectile dysfunction
- Skin aging
- Decreased absorption of vitamin C and folic acid
- Diminished smell and taste sensitivity

ESSENTIAL FACTS

It is important to consider that nicotine from any source (including smokeless tobacco) can affect blood levels of many medications, including theophylline, antico-agulants, beta blockers, calcium channel blockers, and H_2 antagonists.

Health Promotion in Practice

Mr. S smokes a pack of cigarettes a day, but he has not smoked for 6 days while in the hospital. The dose of Coumadin was decreased during his hospitalization and he tells you he will try not to resume smoking. As you prepare him for discharge, you teach him that nicotine can alter the metabolism of Coumadin, and you emphasize that if he resumes smoking he needs to check with his primary care practitioner about the dose of medication.

Involuntary Exposure to Tobacco Smoke

Involuntary exposure to tobacco smoke is called *secondhand tobacco smoke* when it contains smoke that is given off by a burning tobacco product, or is exhaled by someone smoking a tobacco product. *Thirdhand tobacco smoke* refers to the residual pollutants that remain on surfaces (including clothing and hair) after tobacco products have been smoked. Both secondhand and thirdhand smoke are associated with detrimental health effects for nonsmokers. There is no risk-free level of exposure to secondhand smoke, because it increases the risk of premature death and many diseases including lung cancer and cardiovascular disease.

Effects of Smokeless Tobacco

Common types of *smokeless tobacco*—which is any form of tobacco that is not burned—are dip, chew, snuff, oral, and spitting tobacco. These products are placed in the mouth and built-up juices are spit out. Although smokeless tobacco products may be viewed as safe alternatives to smoking, there is no safe form of tobacco. Smokeless tobacco increases the risk of developing tooth loss; heart disease; oral lesions; and oral, esophageal, and pancreatic cancers.

NURSING ASSESSMENT OF RESPIRATORY WELLNESS

Nursing assessment to promote respiratory wellness includes all the following:

- Conditions that threaten respiratory wellness (see Table 14.1)
- Actions the person takes to protect from respiratory illnesses
- For patients who smoke and for those who live with or spend time with someone who smokes: information about pertinent health-related behaviors

One or both of the following assessment tools can be used when assessing patients for respiratory wellness. The first Wellness Assessment Guide is appropriate for all patients and the second Wellness Assessment Guide is applicable for patients who use tobacco products.

ASSESSMENT GUIDE FOR RESPIRATORY WELLNESS

Use the following questions to identify conditions that affect respiratory wellness:

- Do you have any chronic or current problems with breathing?
- Do you have any conditions affecting your respiratory tract (e.g., chronic lung disease, asthma, emphysema, bronchitis)?
- Do you have any allergies affecting your breathing? If so, what are the irritants?
- Have you been exposed or are you currently exposed to respiratory toxins in any of the following situations: military service (e.g., Vietnam), occupations (e.g., coal mining, bar tending), or home (secondhand smoke)?
- Do you engage in hobbies or house maintenance/repair activities that produce dust (e.g., sawing, painting, pottery, woodworking, remodeling with drywall)?
- Do you use any tobacco products (including smokeless), either periodically or regularly? (If yes, use the following Assessment Guide for further assessment.)
- Have you ever used any tobacco products? (If yes, ask about the type, length of time used, length of time since cessation, difficulty of maintaining cessation.)
- How many colds or respiratory infections do you typically have during a year?
- Have you ever had pneumonia?
- Have you ever had tuberculosis or lived with someone who had it?

Use the following questions to assess health-promoting behaviors:

- What do you do to protect yourself from respiratory infections?
- What do you do to protect yourself from secondhand smoke and other environmental toxins?
- Do you get yearly flu immunizations?
- For patients aged 65 and older and people who have chronic conditions: Have you ever had a pneumonia vaccination?
- For patients who engage in activities that produce dust: Do you wear a protective mask or take any other precautions?

ASSESSMENT GUIDE FOR PATIENTS WHO USE TOBACCO PRODUCTS

Ask about patterns of tobacco use: type, frequency, amount used, length of time using tobacco.
Assess level of awareness about effects of tobacco:

- Do you experience any adverse health effects from smoking (or using smokeless tobacco)?
- What potential negative health effects are you aware of with regard to smoking (or using smokeless tobacco)?
- What do you know about the negative effects of smoking on the health of other people?

Assess readiness to quit:

- Have you attempted to quit?
- What are the personal benefits of continuing to smoke?

- What would be the benefits of quitting?
- What supports or resources have you used, or considered using, for quitting smoking?
- On a scale of 1 to 10, with 10 being high, how willing are you to attempt quitting right now?

NURSING INTERVENTIONS TO PROMOTE RESPIRATORY WELLNESS

For all patients, nurses promote respiratory wellness by teaching about protecting oneself from respiratory disease, as summarized in the following Wellness Activity Tool.

Wellness Activity Tool: Actions to Promote Respiratory Wellness

- Sit or stand erect, with head up and shoulders back, to allow optimal lung expansion.
- Several times a day and when in stressful situations, take 10 deep "belly breaths" by fully expanding your abdomen during a long inhalation and then fully exhaling by tightening your abdominal muscles.
- Engage in physical activity for one-half hour daily and include some aerobic activity at least three times weekly.
- Maintain proper weight.
- Drink plenty of fluids.
- Protect from respiratory infections by washing hands frequently, keeping your hands away from your eyes and mouth, and cleaning shared items such as phones with alcohol.
- Avoid exposure to secondhand and thirdhand smoke as much as possible.

- Use a protective mask when engaging in activities that create dust or toxic particles (e.g., sawing).
- Avoid contact with air-borne allergens.
- Use indoor plants to improve air quality in your house.
- If you experience allergies in your home from unavoidable irritants, use an air filter and change or clean the filter as recommended.
- Obtain an influenza immunization every year.
- If you are 65 years or older or have a chronic medical condition, obtain a pneumonia immunization.

ESSENTIAL FACTS

A study by the National Air and Space Association (NASA) found that certain houseplants are very effective in removing air pollutants that are commonly found in homes and offices, such as benzene, formaldehyde, and trichloroethylene.

Health Promotion in Practice

Encourage the use of one or two of the following plants in 6- to 8-inch pots in each room: aloe, dracaena, philodendron, peace lily, snake plant, spider plant, English ivy, bamboo palm, weeping fig, golden pathos, Chinese evergreen.

Talking With Patients About Quitting Smoking

Because of the serious detrimental effects of smoking, education about quitting smoking is a priority for nursing interventions when caring for patients who smoke. Major organizations that emphasize the role of nurses in helping patients quit smoking include the American Nurses Association, the U.S. Department of Health and Human Services, and The Joint Commission on Accreditation of Healthcare Organizations. The following guidelines can be used by nurses and other health care practitioners to help smokers quit. Many excellent resources are available for patient teaching tools and are listed in the ESSENTIAL RESOURCES at the end of this chapter.

HELPING SMOKERS QUIT: A GUIDE FOR CLINICIANS

1. Ask About Tobacco Use at Every Visit
- Implement a system to ensure that tobacco-use status is obtained and recorded at every patient visit as an integral part of vital signs.
- Document tobacco use as current, former, or never.

2. Advise Tobacco Users to Quit
- Use strong, clear, and personalized language.
- "Quitting tobacco is the most important thing you can do to protect your health."

3. Assess Readiness to Quit
- Ask every tobacco user if he/she is willing to quit at this time.
- If willing to quit, provide resources and assistance (as in next step).
- If unwilling to quit at this time, help the patient identify reasons to quit and build the patient's confidence about quitting.

4. Assist Tobacco Users With a Quit Plan
- Help patient establish a plan, including a quit date, removal of tobacco products, obtaining support, and anticipating challenges.

- Give advice about successful quitting.
- Encourage use of recommended medications.

5. *Arrange for Follow-Up Visits*
- Schedule follow-up visits to review progress.

Source: Helping Smokers Quit: A Guide for Clinicians. Revised May 2008. Agency for Healthcare Research and Quality. Rockville, MD. www.ahrq.gov/clinic/tobacco/clinhlpsmksqt.htm

ESSENTIAL FACTS

Recognize that patients who live with or have a caring relationship with someone who smokes may be interested in information about how to support smoking cessation for that person.

Health Promotion in Practice

During a visit with Mrs. S for follow-up on her hypertension, she apologizes about her clothes smelling like cigarette smoke and says she'd really like her husband to quit smoking but she doesn't know where to begin. She is especially concerned about his smoking in the house because their 3-year-old son has had a lot of colds this winter, and she thinks these may be due to her husband's smoking. You suggest she call the National Quitline (1-800-QUITNOW) as a starting point to find out about helpful resources.

Teaching Patients About Breathing Techniques

Simple deep breathing exercises are a health promotion intervention for reducing stress and enhancing respiratory function, when these are done as needed and regularly. The following Wellness Activity Tool can be given to patients to encourage more in-depth self-care exercises on use of breathing for promoting overall wellness.

ESSENTIAL FACTS

Be alert to opportunities to incorporate health education about simple breathing techniques during usual patient care activities.

Health Promotion in Practice

When performing a procedure such as an injection or catheterization, instruct the patient to take deep breaths by expanding his or her belly. Similarly, when assisting with treatments or diagnostic procedures, nurses can facilitate relaxation by both demonstrating and teaching the simple technique for deep breathing.

Wellness Activity Tool: Simple Breathing Technique

When and Where to Do
Use this breathing exercise to generate good energy and to clear your respiratory system. You can do it anywhere, but a quiet and peaceful environment is best. You can do it while walking or standing where you have room to move a full length of your arms.

How to Do
Part I: Tuning Your Senses for Breathing

- Stand with your feet slightly apart or walk on a smooth path during this exercise.
- Call your attention to each of your senses and use the following imagery or develop images that are meaningful to you.
- Visualize your body as a bellows, with your chest expanding and contracting as you breathe in and out.

- Listen to the sound of air as it swishes or swooshes in and out.
- Feel the air as a gentle and refreshing breeze as it moves in and out.
- Smell whatever fragrance conveys the air qualities you want to experience (e.g., fresh, rainy, flowers, evergreens, wheat fields).
- Allow your tongue to feel the air moving across it, and imagine what it might taste like.
- Now focus your attention on your respiratory system.
- Acknowledge your mouth and nose as the gatekeepers of air; appreciate that they allow air to pass in and out.
- With your mouth closed, take a few breaths through your nose and pay attention to how it feels as it passes through your nostrils.
- Hold your nose closed and take a few breaths through your mouth while paying attention to the feel of the air as it passes through.
- Breathe through both your nose and your mouth for the rest of this exercise and appreciate the fullness of the air in and out.

Part II: Repeat the Following Cycle

- Expand your chest and belly as fully as possible while slowly raising both your arms with a flowing movement beginning with your fingertips and involving your shoulders.
- Pull in as much air as you can contain until you feel like you are on the verge of bursting.
- Focus your attention on inviting fresh air to fill your body, your mind, and your spirit—know that you are being inspired.

- Slowly lower your arms to your sides while you squeeze your abdomen and chest wall as tightly as possible to expel as much air as possible.
- Focus your attention on sending all your used and stale air out for dissipation.
- Add different sounds for inspirations and expirations, and listen to the rhythm of the air flowing between you and the universe.

SELF-WELLNESS IN PRACTICE

Take a few minutes to go to a quiet place and do the simple breathing activity described in the Wellness Activity Tool and identify ways of incorporating this during your usual activities.

ESSENTIAL RESOURCES

Tobacco Free Nurses
www.tobaccofreenurses.org
- Articles and other resources related to smoking cessation for nurses and patients
- Links to national organizations and agencies, with an annotated list of recommended sites

Agency for Healthcare Research and Quality
www.ahrq.gov
- Guidelines and teaching tools for health care professionals to help patients quit smoking

American Cancer Society
www.cancer.org
- Information about lung cancer and quitting smoking

American Lung Association
www.lung.org
- Information about lung conditions, tobacco control, and influenza and immunizations

Centers for Disease Control and Prevention
www.cdc.gov
- Information about influenza and respiratory disease and immunizations

National Cancer Institute
www.cancer.gov
- Information about smoking cessation and secondhand smoke

National Heart Lung and Blood Institute
www.nhlbi.nih.gov
- Publications, fact sheets, interactive web applications (e.g., COPD: Learn More Breathe Better)

National Quit Smoking Program
www.smokefree.gov
- National Quitline: 1-800-QUITNOW

Nicotine Anonymous
www.nicotine-anonymous.org
www.Quitsmokeless.org
- Consumer information about quitting smokeless tobacco

Tobacco Information and Prevention Source (TIPS)
www.cdc.gov/tobacco
- Numerous publications and educational materials about all aspects of tobacco (e.g., smoking cessation, health consequences, benefits of quitting, secondhand smoke)

13

Urinary Wellness

Health promotion for urinary wellness focuses on preventing urinary tract disorders and maintaining optimal control over urinary elimination. Health education is especially important in relation to urinary incontinence because there are many misconceptions about this, which lead to inappropriate management strategies. Nurses have important roles in teaching patients about risks that can affect urinary function and actions they can take to promote urinary wellness.

In this chapter, you will learn:

1. How to identify conditions that affect urinary wellness, including medication effects
2. Gender differences and cultural influences in relation to urinary wellness
3. How to assess for conditions affecting urinary wellness, including different types of incontinence
4. How to teach patients about actions to promote good urinary function
5. How to teach patients about urinary incontinence

FACTORS THAT AFFECT URINARY WELLNESS

Many factors can disrupt urinary wellness either chronically or intermittently to increase the risk of urinary retention, incontinence, or urinary tract infection. Although some of these conditions are irreversible, many can be resolved—or at least improved—through health promotion interventions, as discussed later in this chapter. It is important to recognize that some conditions are caused by false perceptions, which can be addressed through patient teaching interventions. For example, urinary incontinence is often viewed as an inevitable consequence of aging. In reality, age-related changes do not cause urinary incontinence in healthy adults, but they can exacerbate the effects of other conditions that increase the risk of urinary incontinence.

RISK ASSESSMENT TOOL: CONDITIONS THAT CAN AFFECT URINARY WELLNESS

Conditions That Increase the Risk of Urinary Incontinence

- Functional limitations, especially those that affect mobility, extremities, fine motor movement, or any aspect of toileting
- Smoking
- Constipation
- Obesity
- Consumption of foods and beverages that irritate the bladder or stimulate diuresis (alcohol, caffeinated or carbonated drinks, citric juices, artificial sweeteners)

- Inadequate fluid intake
- Medical conditions (e.g., neurologic conditions, diabetes, urinary tract infection)
- Cognitive impairment

Conditions in Women

- Loss of muscle tone from childbearing
- Engagement in high-impact sports such as gymnastics, softball, volleyball, or basketball
- Hormonal changes due to pregnancy or menopause
- Pelvic organ prolapse (also called vaginal prolapse)
- Gynecologic surgery

Conditions in Men

- History of prostate surgery
- History of radiation therapy, or urethral or pelvic trauma

Age-Related Changes
That Affect Urinary Wellness

- Changes in diurnal production of urine, with greater quantities at night
- Diminished bladder capacity
- Diminished tone and strength of the external urinary sphincter
- Delayed sensation of bladder fullness
- Diminished efficiency of bladder emptying

Conditions That Increase the Risk of Bladder Cancer

- Being White, male, older than 40 years
- Smoking cigarettes, cigars, or pipes
- Occupational exposure to diesel fumes and chemicals in synthetic dyes, paint, printing, rubber, leather, textile, and hairdressing industries and products
- Synergistic effect of smoking and occupational exposure to toxins
- Chronic bladder irritation or infections
- Personal or family history of bladder cancer
- Chemotherapy with cyclophosphamide (Cytoxan)

Environmental Factors Associated With Urinary Incontinence

Because access to acceptable toileting facilities is imperative for maintaining continence, environmental barriers can have a significant influence on people who are predisposed to urinary incontinence. For example, people with limited mobility often encounter physical barriers, such as stairs, narrow doorways, double doors, and heavy doors that are difficult to open. People with visual–perceptual limitations may have difficulty finding facilities, even those that are physically accessible.

Medication Effects on Urinary Function

Adverse effects of medications can affect urinary function in many ways, as delineated by the examples in Table 13.1.

TABLE 13.1 Effects of Medications on Urinary Wellness

Medication	Effect on Urinary Wellness
Diuretics	Urinary frequency, urgency
Medications with cholinergic actions (e.g., bethanechol)	Increased bladder contractions, causing urgency, frequency, incontinence
Alpha-adrenergic blockers (e.g., terazosin)	Relaxation of urinary muscles, causing urinary incontinence
Beta-adrenergic blockers (e.g., propranolol)	Urinary incontinence due to sphincter relaxation
Alpha-adrenergic agonists (e.g., pseudoephedrine) or calcium-channel blockers	Overflow incontinence
Anticholinergic medications (e.g., antihistamines, antidepressants, prescription or nonprescription eyedrops or medications for colds or allergies)	Urinary retention, especially in the presence of prostatic hypertrophy (for men)

ESSENTIAL FACTS

Recognize that medications can have a synergistic effect to significantly increase the risk of adverse effects.

Health Promotion in Practice

Mr. N has been taking propranolol (Inderal) for angina for many years. He recently started taking terazosin (Hytrin) for benign prostatic hyperplasia and reports, "I used to have a little dribbling and some trouble starting my stream, but now I have less control over my urine." You suggest that he talk with his primary care practitioner about this change and ask if it might be associated with his medications.

Gender Differences

Gender differences influence urinary wellness in several ways. Anatomically, the female urethra is about one-fifth the length of the male urethra, so women have less control over the external sphincter. This difference partially explains the increased susceptibility of women to urinary incontinence when other risk factors are present. In addition, anatomical differences in the proximity of the female urethra to the anus account for some of the increased susceptibility of women to urinary tract infections. Thus, for women, sexual intercourse and incorrect wiping after bowel movements are activities that can increase the risk of introducing pathological organisms into the urinary meatus.

Cultural Influences

In clinical settings, it is important to be aware of cultural factors that can affect behaviors associated with toileting, as in the following examples of culturally based variations in toileting preferences (Lipson & Dibble, 2005):

- Privacy is imperative, especially for using a commode, bedpan, or urinal.
- If assistance is needed, having someone of the same gender is preferable.
- It is essential to wash the genital area with soap and water or in a bidet after voiding.
- Squatting is the usual position for voiding.
- Elimination is not done at prayer time.
- Use of bathroom, rather than bedpan or bedside commode, is necessary for comfort, privacy, and to prevent inconvenience for caregivers.
- Bedpans, urinals, and all toileting equipment must be kept covered.

• The left hand is used to wash and wipe after toileting.
• The bedpan or urinal must be away from the person's upper body.
• The patient may be reluctant to save urine for measuring or testing because of modesty.

NURSING ASSESSMENT OF URINARY WELLNESS

From a health promotion perspective, nurses assess all of the following aspects of urinary function:

• The patient's perception of urinary function
• Problems with control over urination
• Risks of urinary incontinence, urinary tract infections, or bladder cancer
• Health-promoting behaviors that promote urinary wellness

Use the following Wellness Assessment Guide to identify conditions of the urinary tract that need to be addressed through nursing interventions.

ASSESSMENT GUIDE FOR URINARY WELLNESS

Ask these questions to assess overall urinary function:

• About how many times a day do you go to the bathroom for urinating?
• How many times do you get up during the night to go to the bathroom?
• Do you have a history of kidney or bladder stones?

- Do you have a history of urinary tract infections? (If yes, ask about frequency, last one, etc.)
- Do you have any problems with constipation?
- Do you experience leaking of urine before you can get to the toilet? (If yes, ask additional questions about burning, urgency, frequency, postvoid dribbling, having to exert unusual pressure on your bladder for complete emptying)
- Do you use pads, briefs, or other products to manage incontinence?

Men Only
- Do you have any difficulty starting the stream or keeping it going?
- Have you ever been told you had (or been checked for) prostate problems?
- Have you had any surgery for prostate or bladder problems?

Women Only
- Have you had any children? (If yes, ask how many, what methods of delivery, etc.)
- Have you had any "female" surgery (e.g., pelvic or bladder repair)?
- Have you had any vaginal infections? (If yes, ask about types, frequency, etc.)

Use these questions to assess health-related behaviors that affect urinary wellness:

- What is your usual amount and type of daily fluid intake?
- How much and how often do you drink caffeinated beverages?
- Are you familiar with Kegel (or pelvic floor muscle) exercises and do you ever perform them?

Ask the following questions to identify risks of bladder cancer:

- Do you smoke or use any tobacco or nicotine products?
- How much alcohol do you drink?
- Do you have a history of any conditions that cause chronic bladder inflammations (e.g., recurrent infections, kidney or bladder stones)?
- Have you worked in any occupation where you were exposed to toxins such as dyes or diesel fuel (e.g., printing, painting, textiles, rubber, hairdressing, truck driving)? If yes, what kind of workplace precautions did your employer enforce?
- Do you have a personal or family history of bladder cancer?
- Have you received radiation treatments to your pelvic area?
- Have you been treated with cyclophosphamide (Cytoxan) for cancer?

Incorporate the following information to assess urinary wellness:

- Medications that can affect urinary function (refer to Table 13.1)
- Conditions that affect access to toileting facilities (e.g., mobility problems, difficulty with manual dexterity, visual impairments)
- Risks of urinary tract infections (e.g., diabetes, use of diaphragms for birth control, conditions or medications that suppress immune function)

Identifying Different Types of Incontinence

If patients have symptoms of urinary incontinence (i.e., involuntary release of urine), it is important to find out whether this problem is chronic, intermittent, or recent onset. Regardless of the duration of the problem, however, assess the patient's understanding of it and find out whether the patient has had any evaluation to identify causative factors and potential treatment options. Types of urinary incontinence are:

- *Stress:* Occurring during activities that cause increased intra-abdominal pressure (coughing, laughing)
- *Urge:* Occurring soon after a strong sensation of urgency to void
- *Mixed:* Having symptoms of both stress and urge incontinence
- *Functional:* Due to inability to get to the toilet in time to avoid unintentional urination, usually associated with physical disability
- *Overflow:* Associated with overdistension of the bladder, usually associated with neurologic problems affecting control over urination
- *Reflex:* Occurring at somewhat predictable intervals when specific volume is reached
- *Total:* Large volumes, occurring continuously or unpredictably

Since 1997, the term *overactive bladder (OAB)* has been used to describe "urgency," with or without urge incontinence, usually with frequency and nocturia in the absence of an underlying metabolic or pathologic condition (Wein, 2011). Because of widespread advertising related to OAB, this condition is commonly perceived as easily cured with medications. However, it is important to know that symptoms of other conditions, including prostatic enlargement, urinary tract infections, and bladder cancer, are similar to those of OAB, so a thorough medical evaluation is imperative. Additional points to teach patients about OAB are that medications are not always effective and may have adverse effects and that nonpharmaco-logical interventions are important for urge or mixed incontinence (Agency for Healthcare Research and Quality, 2012).

ESSENTIAL FACTS

Be aware of terminology and focus on using positive phrases, such as "maintaining control," rather than negative phrases, such as "accidents." Also, use terms such as "briefs" rather than "diapers" in reference to incontinence products.

NURSING INTERVENTIONS TO PROMOTE URINARY WELLNESS

From a health promotion perspective, nursing interventions for urinary wellness address all the following:

- Obtaining help from appropriate professionals for urinary incontinence
- Identifying risks for conditions affecting the urinary tract
- Correcting inaccurate perceptions about urinary incontinence
- Using self-care practices to promote optimal urinary continence

Teaching Patients About Self-Care Actions for Urinary Wellness

For all patients, health promotion for urinary wellness focuses on self-care actions to promote optimal urinary function, as summarized in the following Wellness Activity Tool.

Wellness Activity Tool for Promoting Optimal Urinary Function

Actions to Promote Good Urinary Function
- Drink between 7.5 and 10 eight-ounce glasses of water and other noncaffeinated beverages daily.
- Limit intake of food and beverages that can cause urinary retention, urgency, or frequency, such as those that are high in sodium, foods that are spicy or contain artificial sweeteners, and caffeinated or carbonated beverages.
- Maintain a healthy weight because obesity increases the risk of developing urinary incontinence.
- Engage in regular physical activity to prevent many of the conditions that are risk factors for urinary incontinence.
- Include adequate fiber in the diet and maintain good bowel function to prevent constipation, which is a risk factor for urinary incontinence.
- Do not smoke or drink excessive amounts of alcohol to reduce the risk for bladder cancer.
- Obtain an evaluation from your primary care practitioner if symptoms of urinary problems develop.

Women Only
- Use good hygiene practices for perineal area, such as wiping from front to back after bowel movements.
- Wear underwear with a cotton crotch.

- Drink water, emptying bladder, and maintain good perineal hygiene after sexual intercourse.
- Do not use deodorant sprays or other feminine products around the perineal area.
- Do not take bubble baths.

Men Only
- Use a condom during intercourse to reduce the risk of urinary tract infections.
- Use good hygiene practices for urethral area, including washing carefully under foreskin if uncircumcised.

Teaching Patients About Control Over Urination

From a health promotion perspective, nurses have important roles in correcting myths and misunderstandings about urinary incontinence, especially when patients view this as an untreatable condition or an inevitable consequence of aging, childbirth, or other conditions. Thus, a major focus is encouraging patients to discuss their symptoms with their primary care practitioner and offering a sense of hope that incontinence can be resolved or at least improved. Another major focus of health promotion is teaching about *pelvic floor muscle exercises* (also called *Kegels*), which is now widely recognized as an evidence-based self-care intervention for improving control over urination for men and women who have urge, stress, or mixed incontinence. The following Wellness Activity Tool can be given to patients who are experiencing any form of incontinence. The ESSENTIAL RESOURCES lists sources of excellent patient teaching materials pertinent to bladder health and urinary incontinence.

========================= *ESSENTIAL FACTS*

Address all contributing factors with the goal of resolving or improving incontinence before managing the problem with disposable products.

Health Promotion in Practice

Mrs. K is being discharged to a rehabilitation facility following knee replacement surgery, and she asks for "pads for my panties because I never needed anything before but now I've got some leakage and I've had some problems holding my water during therapy." She had an indwelling catheter for 3 days during her hospitalization, but has not been evaluated for a urinary tract infection. You obtain an order for a urinalysis and emphasize that Mrs. K needs to request further evaluation of the recent-onset urinary incontinence.

Wellness Activity Tool: Tips on Maintaining Urinary Continence

Facts About Urinary Incontinence

- Because many different conditions can cause difficulty controlling urination (i.e., incontinence), it is imperative to have this evaluated by a health care professional so the most appropriate interventions can be initiated.
- Although aging increases the chance of developing urinary incontinence, it is not an inevitable outcome of aging, nor should it be viewed as untreatable at any age.
- Conditions that affect one's ability to control urination include obesity, constipation,

medications (e.g., diuretics), functional limitations, pathologic conditions (e.g., dementia, diabetes, urinary tract infections), history of prostatectomy or gynecologic surgery, pelvic organ prolapse, and loss of pelvic muscle tone (e.g., from childbirth or decreased estrogen).
- Pelvic floor muscle exercises, also known as Kegels, are one of the most effective ways of improving or alleviating stress and mixed urinary incontinence.
- Additional nonpharmacologic interventions for improving incontinence include weight loss and exercise, biofeedback, bladder training, and magnetic, electrical, or percutaneous tibial nerve stimulation.
- Some types of incontinence may improve with medications, but the treatment must be matched appropriately with the problem, and it is important to observe for adverse medication effects.

How to Do Pelvic Floor Muscle Exercises

Women: Identify the proper muscles by placing your finger in your vagina and squeezing enough to feel pressure.

Men: Identify the proper muscles by sitting comfortably with your abdominal muscles relaxed; then squeeze your pelvic muscles as if you are trying to stop the flow of urine or the passage of gas.

- Relax your back, thighs, and abdomen so you can concentrate on the pelvic floor muscles.
- Lie on your back or sit with your knees together and squeeze your pelvic floor muscle.
- Hold the contraction for 3 to 4 seconds, and then relax the muscle for 3 to 4 seconds.
- Repeat this cycle for 5 minutes twice a day.

- Try to gradually lengthen the time until you can hold each contraction and relaxation for 8 seconds.
- After you have mastered this technique, try doing the exercises while standing or with your knees apart.
- Continue performing these exercises for 5 minutes twice a day until you have regained control over your urination, then maintain the improvement by performing them for 5 minutes three times a week.
- Perform these exercises for 6 to 12 weeks to notice an improvement in bladder control.

SELF-WELLNESS IN PRACTICE

If you experience episodes of urinary urgency or incontinence, practice pelvic muscle exercises, and try to identify conditions that can cause these episodes, such as certain foods, beverages, medications, or constipation.

ESSENTIAL RESOURCES

American Foundation for Urologic Disease
www.urologyhealth.org

National Association for Continence
www.nafc.org

Simon Foundation for Continence
www.simonfoundation.org

Society for Urological Nurse Associates (SUNA)
www.suna.org

Wound, Ostomy, and Continence Nurses (WOCN)
www.wocn.org

14

Visual Wellness

Vision changes are one of the earliest signs of aging and even the healthiest people need some magnifying lenses—such as nonprescription reading glasses—by the time they are 50 years of age. Independent of age-related changes, however, many variables affect one's ability to see, and some of these can be addressed through health promotion interventions. For example, type and amount of lighting are major factors that affect visual function for all people. Health promotion interventions for all adults focus on protecting their vision and on maintaining optimal visual abilities.

In this chapter, you will learn:

1. Conditions that affect vision or cause vision loss
2. How to assess visual wellness
3. Interventions to promote visual wellness

177

FACTORS THAT AFFECT VISION

Factors that affect vision can be categorized as age-related changes, pathologic conditions, adverse medication effects, and type and amount of lighting. An important consideration with regard to risks for vision impairment is the degree to which they can be addressed through health promotion interventions, as delineated in the Risk Assessment Tool.

RISK ASSESSMENT TOOL: CONDITIONS THAT CAN AFFECT VISUAL WELLNESS

Conditions That Respond to Health Promotion Interventions

- Smoking
- Type and amount of lighting
- Exposure to sunlight
- Risk of injury
- Intense and uninterrupted focusing on computer or video screens

Conditions That Are Addressed by Primary Care Practitioners

- Pathologic conditions of the eye (e.g., glaucoma, cataracts, retinopathy)
- Pathologic conditions of other systems that affect vision (e.g., stroke, diabetes, hypertension)
- Dry eyes

Adverse Medication Effects

- Increased risk for development of cataracts, glaucoma, and macular degeneration (see Table 14.1 for examples)

- Dry eyes: estrogen, diuretics, antihistamines, anticholinergics, phenothiazines, beta-blockers, and antiparkinson agents

Conditions That Cannot Be Changed

- Heredity
- Age-related changes affecting the eyes and visual processing
- Long-term detrimental effects of sunlight and toxins

ESSENTIAL FACTS

It is important to identify risk factors that can be modified through simple self-care actions.

Health Promotion in Practice

It is relatively easy to protect oneself from sunlight by wearing sunglasses, and to prevent eye strain by frequently blinking and looking in another direction when focusing intensely on a computer screen.

VISION CHANGES AND IMPAIRMENT

Presbyopia is the age-related vision change that affects most people by the age of 50 years and manifests in the following ways:

- Difficulty focusing on close objects, such as small print
- Increased sensitivity to glare
- Diminished depth perception
- Slower adaptive response when moving from a dark to a brightly lit environment

- Narrower visual field
- Difficulty distinguishing colors, especially in the blue-green or yellow-white ranges
- Slower processing of visual images

Cataracts, glaucoma, and macular degeneration are the most common causes of vision impairment in adults. Table 14.1 delineates effects of and risk factors for these conditions.

TABLE 14.1 Characteristics of Cataracts, Glaucoma, and Macular Degeneration

Condition	Effects on Vision	Risk Factors
Cataracts	Gradual onset of blurred or double vision, distorted images, decreased contrast sensitivity, increased sensitivity to glare, altered color perception, and frequent changes of corrective lenses	Advanced age, smoking, diabetes, malnutrition, exposure to sunlight, adverse medication effects (e.g., corticosteroids, phenothiazines, amiodarone, benzodiazepines, cholinesterase inhibitors)
Glaucoma	Chronic: gradual onset, increased sensitivity to glare, difficulty seeing in dim light, decreased contrast sensitivity, narrower perceptual field Acute: sudden onset of intense pain and blurred vision, nausea, vomiting, and seeing halos around lights	Advanced age, diabetes, African American race, family history, adverse medication effects (e.g., corticosteroids and anticholinergics)
Macular degeneration	Blurred vision, gradual and progressive loss of central vision, and perception of straight lines as crooked	Advanced age, smoking, hypertension, hyperlipidemia, non-Hispanic White ethnicity, family history, adverse medication effects (e.g., tamoxifen, phenothiazines, chloroquine)

ESSENTIAL FACTS

It is important to recognize the difference between effects of age-related changes and symptoms of an eye disease that warrant medical treatment.

Health Promotion in Practice

Mrs. V, who is a 67-year-old African American with diabetes, reports that she sees halos around streetlights and has been needing more light for household tasks. When she attributes these changes to "getting older" you ask if she has had her eyes checked and you suggest that these symptoms could be related to a treatable eye disease rather than to age-related changes.

NURSING ASSESSMENT OF VISUAL WELLNESS

In clinical settings, it is important to determine whether a patient has any vision impairment that needs to be addressed in the care plan. Nursing assessment of visual wellness also focuses on identifying vision changes that warrant further evaluation and risk factors that affect visual wellness.

GUIDE TO NURSING ASSESSMENT OF VISUAL FUNCTION

Ask these questions to assess overall visual wellness:

• Do you usually wear eyeglasses or contact lenses? (If yes, are they accessible and is the patient able to use them?)
• On a scale of 1 to 10, with 10 being perfect, how would you rate your vision in your left (right) eye, when you are wearing corrective lenses (if prescribed)?

- Have you noticed any changes in your ability to see, either during close-vision tasks such as reading or sewing, or when you are looking farther than 20 feet?
- Do you experience any uncomfortable symptoms, such as dryness, itching, or excessive tearing?
- Do you have difficulty performing any of your usual activities, like driving at night, because you have trouble seeing?
- Have you ever tripped or fallen because of trouble seeing?

Ask these questions to identify risks for vision problems:

- Do you smoke cigarettes?
- Do you have any family history of eye conditions, especially glaucoma or macular degeneration?
- Are you frequently exposed to environmental or occupational conditions that irritate your eyes or seem to cause dryness?
- Do you have a history of diabetes or hypertension?

Ask the following questions to assess health-promoting behaviors:

- Do you protect your eyes when you are out in the sun?
- When was the last time you had your eyes checked?
- Where do you go for eye care?
- (If the patient is 40 years or older) Have you ever had your eyes checked for glaucoma or other conditions that can affect your vision?

Incorporate the following observations that are pertinent to visual functioning:

- Check for sources of glare that can be reduced.
- Observe whether the lighting is optimal and identify adjustments that can be made.

- Can the patient read printed materials?
- Can the patient accurately describe an object that is more than 20 feet away?

 *ESSENTIAL FACTS*

During an initial assessment when patients are admitted to the hospital, it is important to ask if they use prescription eyedrops because this is an easily overlooked, but very important, aspect of health care.

NURSING INTERVENTIONS TO PROMOTE VISUAL WELLNESS

Nurses have opportunities to promote visual wellness for patients through actions such as the following:

- Adjust lighting as much as possible by providing adequate nonglare lighting from several sources and avoiding sharp contrasts in lighting.
- Make sure eyeglasses are accessible for patients who use them.
- Provide necessary assistance to keep eyeglasses clean and care for contact lenses.
- If a patient usually uses contact lenses but cannot wear them, talk with the patient or family about obtaining eyeglasses.
- When caring for or talking with patients, avoid standing in front of bright or glaring light.
- Request a referral for occupational therapy if magnifiers or other low-vision aids would be beneficial.

ESSENTIAL FACTS

Pay attention to environmental conditions and take simple actions to improve vision for patients.

Health Promotion in Practice

Mr. I's hospital bed is positioned parallel to a south-facing window. When staff come to talk with him during bright daylight hours, they stand on the side of the bed away from the window so glare does not interfere with his ability to see their faces.

Teaching Patients About Health Promotion for Visual Wellness

Teaching about health promotion for visual wellness focuses on self-care actions to protect vision, including detection of eye diseases at an early stage, as summarized in the following Wellness Teaching Tool. When caring for patients who have a disease that affects their vision (e.g., glaucoma, cataracts, or macular degeneration), it is important to teach about resources for reliable information about vision changes, such as the ones listed in the ESSENTIAL RESOURCES at the end of this chapter.

Wellness Teaching Tool: Promoting Visual Wellness

Actions to Protect Your Vision
- If you are 40 years or older, get a comprehensive dilated eye exam at least every 2 years.
- Obtain a medical evaluation if you notice any changes in vision, especially sudden ones.
- Wear sunglasses that block out 99% to 100% of both UV-A and UV-B radiation whenever you are in the sunlight.
- If you smoke, quit.

- Wear a broad-brimmed hat to protect from sunlight.
- Wear eye protection when working with chemical substances that are liquid or emit toxic fumes (e.g., ammonia-based cleaning supplies).
- Wear eye protection when using power tools or engaging in risky sports or other activities.
- Include at least five servings of fruits and vegetable in the daily diet.
- Include foods that are rich in omega-3 fatty acids to protect from macular degeneration.
- If you focus intensely on a computer screen, frequently blink and look in a different direction.

SELF-WELLNESS IN PRACTICE

Develop the habit of always wearing sunglasses whenever you are outside or in a vehicle during daylight hours.

ESSENTIAL RESOURCES

American Foundation for the Blind
www.afb.org

Eye Care America
www.eyecareamerica.org

Glaucoma Foundation
www.glaucomafoundation.org

Lighthouse International
www.lighthouse.org

Lions Club International
www.lionsclubs.org

National Eye Institute
www.nei.nih.gov/healthyeyes

Prevent Blindness America
www.preventblindness.org

15

Hearing Wellness

A certain amount of hearing loss occurs with normal aging, but many conditions not only exacerbate the effects of age-related changes, but also independently cause hearing loss in adults of all ages. For example, noise-induced hearing loss is one of the most common causes of hearing loss and it is a major focus of health promotion because it can be prevented. For all patients it is important to address modifiable conditions that affect hearing, and for people with hearing loss it is imperative to focus on interventions to improve auditory communication.

In this chapter, you will learn:

1. Conditions that interfere with hearing or cause hearing loss
2. How to assess hearing loss and identify conditions that can be addressed through health promotion
3. Techniques for communicating effectively with people who have hearing loss
4. How to teach patients about actions they can take to promote hearing wellness

FACTORS THAT AFFECT HEARING WELLNESS

Most adults notice some hearing loss by the time they are in their 60s due to normal age-related changes. Regardless of age, however, many hearing impairments can be prevented or delayed by addressing environmental, lifestyle, or other modifiable causative conditions. The following Risk Assessment Tool identifies conditions that affect hearing according to the potential for addressing these conditions.

RISK ASSESSMENT TOOL: CONDITIONS THAT CAN AFFECT HEARING WELLNESS

Conditions That Respond to Health Promotion Interventions

- Exposure to noise
- Cigarette smoking
- Impacted wax
- Communication techniques

Conditions That Are Addressed by Primary Care Practitioners

- Adverse medication effects
- Acute or chronic medical conditions (e.g., ear infections, diabetes, neurologic conditions)

Conditions That Cannot Be Changed

- Hereditary hearing loss (e.g., otosclerosis)
- Age-related changes affecting the auditory system
- Scarring of the tympanic membrane

- Damage to the auditory organs due to trauma (e.g., head injury)
- Pathologic conditions affecting the auditory system (e.g., syphilis, Ménière's disease, neurologic conditions)
- Damage from toxins, including cigarette smoking and occupational exposure to chemicals

HEARING LOSS

Hearing loss is categorized according to the site of the pathologic damage as follows:

- *Conductive* hearing loss is associated with conditions of the outer and middle parts of the ear, such as impacted wax or scarring or perforation of the tympanic membrane.
- *Sensorineural* hearing loss is caused by damage to the nerve pathways and the organs of the inner ear. Conditions that most often are associated with sensorineural loss are age-related changes (*presbycusis*), heredity (*otosclerosis*), trauma, pathologic conditions, adverse medication effects, toxins (e.g., cigarette smoking), and exposure to noise (*noise-induced hearing loss*).
- If the hearing loss involves both conductive and sensorineural impairments, it is called a *mixed hearing loss*.

Two characteristics of sounds that significantly affect one's ability to hear are intensity and frequency. *Intensity*, which is measured in *decibels*, describes the loudness or softness of a sound. This characteristic is important in identifying conditions that can cause noise-induced hearing loss. *Frequency,* which is measured in *hertz,* refers to whether a sound is high- or low-pitched. In general, vowels are lower pitched and consonants higher pitched. This characteristic is pertinent when considering the effect of different types of hearing impairments. For example, sensorineural impairments initially affect one's ability to hear high-pitched sounds, so the earliest sign of this type of hearing loss is difficulty understanding words that are rich in sibilants (e.g., *ch, f, s, sh, t, th,* and *w*). Someone with a sensorineural hearing loss would have difficulty understanding a sentence like "She wished she would fish on Thursday" but have less difficulty with a sentence such as "Pam wanted to go boating on Monday."

Noise-Induced Hearing Loss

Noise-induced hearing loss is an important focus of health promotion because it accounts for half of the cases of hearing impairment and is considered 100% preventable (National Institute on Deafness and Other Communication Disorders, 2008; Oishi & Schacht, 2011). Noise-induced hearing loss can be caused by exposure to sounds at or above 85 decibels, either intermittently (e.g., explosion, fireworks) or ongoing, as in occupational or recreational activities. The following Risk Assessment Tool can be used to increase patient awareness of common sources of noise that exceed the recommended safe levels.

RISK ASSESSMENT TOOL: CAUSES OF NOISE-INDUCED HEARING LOSS

Household Items That Typically Exceed Safe Noise Levels

- Hairdryer, dishwasher, vacuum cleaner
- Small kitchen appliances: blender, mixer, coffee grinder, food processor, electric can opener
- Power tools: saws, drills, blowers, lawn and garden equipment

Recreational Sources of Harmful Noise

- Live or recorded music when loud or played directly into the ears
- Boat motors, motorcycles
- Firecrackers, firearms, hunting, target shooting

Occupational Groups at High-Risk of Hearing Loss

- Miners, farmers
- Plumbers, carpenters, construction workers
- Musicians and sound engineers
- Armed services members
- Firefighters and emergency service workers

Ototoxic Medications

Ototoxicity is the tendency of a substance to damage the inner ear structures, potentially causing hearing loss. More than 700 medications are known to be ototoxic when administered orally or in other ways, such as rectally or intravenously (Bisht & Bist, 2011). Examples of ototoxic medications are loop diuretics; beta blockers; nonsteroidal anti-inflammatory drugs; platinum compounds for cancer chemotherapy; and aminoglycoside, macrolide, and quinolone antibiotics.

═══════════════ *ESSENTIAL FACTS*

Be aware of potential relationships between medications and hearing loss, particularly in people who have additional risks for hearing loss.

Health Promotion in Practice

Mr. R is a retired miner who smokes a pack of cigarettes a day and takes furosemide and metoprolol. When he says, "I have a hard time hearing what you say because you talk too softly," you recognize that he has several conditions that increase his risk for hearing loss. Your response is "There are many reasons why you could be having a hard time hearing me, so it would be good to ask your doctor about your hearing problem because some of these conditions could be addressed."

NURSING ASSESSMENT OF HEARING WELLNESS

In clinical settings, it is important to determine whether a patient has a hearing deficit that interferes with communication. From a health promotion perspective, a nursing assessment of hearing wellness includes all the following aspects:

• Simple tests for even mild hearing loss
• Identifying risks for hearing impairment
• Identifying the patient's readiness to address his or her hearing loss
• Identifying the patient's attitudes about the hearing loss and use of hearing aids

The following guide can be used to assess these aspects.

ASSESSMENT GUIDE FOR HEARING WELLNESS

Ask these questions to identify risk factors for hearing loss:

• Do you have a family history of hearing loss or deafness?
• Have you been exposed to loud noise in your job or leisure activities, or do you currently engage in any activities that expose you to loud noise?
• Have you been exposed to workplace toxins, such as fuels, metals, or toluene?
• When you engage in activities that involve the use of noisy equipment, do you use ear protectors?
• Do you smoke cigarettes? (If yes, do you realize that this is a risk factor for hearing loss?)
• Have you ever had impacted wax in your ears? (If yes, ask about frequency, last ear check, actions to prevent or treat.)

Use the following questions to assess usual hearing abilities:

• On a scale of 1 to 10, with 10 being perfect, how would you rate your hearing in your left (right) ear?
• Have you noticed any change in your ability to understand conversations or hear words?
• Do you have any trouble hearing if people whisper or speak in a low voice?
• Do you turn the volume up higher than usual (or do other people complain that you do) when you listen to the radio, television, or music?
• Are you bothered by any abnormal noise in your ears, such as ringing or buzzing?
• Do you experience hypersensitivity to noise, or are you bothered by noises that don't seem to bother other people?

Observe for any of the following behaviors that are indicative of hearing loss:

- Inappropriate responses to questions, especially in the absence of opportunities for lip reading
- Frequent requests for repetition or clarification of verbal communication
- Intensely focusing on your face, mouthing your words, turning one ear toward you
- Speaking loudly or inarticulately

Ask the following questions if the person is aware of having a hearing loss:

- How does your hearing problem affect your daily life?
- Are there any activities that you would like to do but don't do because of hearing limitations?
- Have you ever had, or considered having, an evaluation for a hearing aid? (What concerns do you have that keep you from having an evaluation?)
- Do you have a hearing aid that you are not using now? If yes, what is the reason you are not using it?

ESSENTIAL FACTS

Because risk factors for hearing impairment can have a synergistic effect, it is important to identify combinations of conditions. For example, someone who smokes cigarettes and is exposed to noise in the workplace has a significantly increased risk of hearing impairment in contrast to a nonsmoker in the same workplace (Mohammadi, Mazhari, Mehrparvar, & Attarchi, 2010).

NURSING INTERVENTIONS TO PROMOTE HEARING WELLNESS

Because impacted wax is a readily treated cause of hearing loss, it is important to check ear canals and initiate interventions if appropriate. Another intervention for patients who have a hearing loss is to use communication techniques that are effective for that person. Use the following guidelines for communicating with someone who has a hearing loss:

- Provide good, nonglare lighting.
- If applicable, make sure the person is wearing clean eyeglasses and using hearing aids.
- Eliminate all background noise as much as possible.
- Position yourself directly in front of the person.
- Make sure you have the person's attention before beginning to talk.
- Maintain good face-to-face contact; do not cover your mouth or chew gum.
- Speak distinctly, slowly, and directly to the person, but do not use exaggerated mouth movements.
- Speak in a moderately loud voice but do not raise the tone of your voice.
- Early in the interaction, ask the person if you are speaking at the best level of loudness and adjust accordingly.
- Use body language and written communication to reinforce your message.
- At appropriate intervals, ask for feedback to ascertain the person's understanding.
- Avoid asking questions that elicit simple yes or no responses because it is more difficult to evaluate the person's understanding.
- If the person has trouble understanding, repeat the message with different words (e.g., substitute words with different sounds).

ESSENTIAL FACTS

When communicating with a patient who has significant hearing loss and does not have his or her hearing aids, find out if an assistive listening device is available. For example, the clinic or hospital may have a personal amplification device to facilitate communication with patients.

Teaching Patients About Health Promotion for Hearing Wellness

Health promotion for all patients focuses on teaching about relatively simple self-care actions to protect their hearing. For patients with any degree of hearing loss, include information about appropriate evaluation and management interventions, as described in the following Wellness Activity Tool. Another intervention is to encourage patients to find additional information from the sources listed in the ESSENTIAL RESOURCES at the end of this chapter.

Wellness Activity Tool: Promoting Hearing Wellness

Actions to Protect Your Hearing
- Limit your exposure to any noise that is louder than 85 decibels (e.g., motorcycles, lawn mowers, chainsaws, powerboats, music when played loudly).
- A simple indicator of noise that is too loud: if you have to raise your voice to be heard above the noise by someone within an arm's length away.
- When you cannot avoid exposure to noise, use ear protectors that are appropriate for the task.

- Because smoking increases the risk of hearing loss, consider quitting if you smoke.
- Have your ears checked for impacted wax and use preventive measures as necessary.

Actions to Take if You Have a Hearing Loss
- Discuss this with your primary care practitioner to determine whether there is an underlying medical condition or whether the impairment might be an adverse medication effect.
- Recognize that some hearing loss is a normal consequence of aging, but many modifiable conditions increase the risk of hearing loss and should be addressed.
- Because many types of hearing aids are available, obtain an evaluation from a professional who is not selling one particular type of hearing aid.
- Speech and hearing centers, which are often associated with universities or medical centers, are reliable sources for evaluation and recommendations about hearing devices.
- If you need financial support for hearing aids, contact *Self Help for Hard of Hearing People* (www.hearingloss.org) for information.
- Consider using amplifying devices (e.g., for phone, radios, doorbells) or sound-substitution devices (e.g., flashing lights) for improving safety in daily life.

SELF-WELLNESS IN PRACTICE

Develop the habit of listening to your environment and being aware of the many sources of extraneous noise so you can eliminate those that are potentially harmful.

ESSENTIAL RESOURCES

Better Hearing Institute
www.betterhearing.org

Hear-It
www.hear-it.org

International Hearing Society
www.ihsinfo.org

National Hearing Conservation Association
www.hearingconservation.org

National Institute on Deafness and Other Communication Disorders
www.nidcd.nih.gov

National Institute for Occupational Safety and Health
www.cdc.gov/niosh

Noise Free America
www.noisefree.org

Noise OFF
www.NoiseOFF.org

Noise Pollution Clearinghouse
www.nonoise.org

16

Sexual Wellness

Although the topic of sexual wellness is associated with privacy, embarrassment, and strong emotions, sexuality is an integral aspect of one's personhood that has many implications for health promotion. Nurses are not expected to be experts about all topics associated with sexual function, but they have important roles in discussing pertinent issues and suggesting appropriate resources. This chapter is intended to increase nurses' comfort level in discussing concerns pertinent to sexual wellness and to provide basic information about resources for addressing these needs.

In this chapter, you will learn:

1. Identifying beliefs and attitudes pertinent to promoting sexual wellness
2. When and how to talk with patients about sexual wellness
3. Resources for addressing patient needs related to sexual wellness

BECOMING COMFORTABLE WITH THE TOPIC

Perhaps the best way to become comfortable with discussing sexual wellness in patient care settings is to view it in the same context as other aspects that are considered private but important to overall health. For example, urinary incontinence and some mental health conditions are topics that are associated with embarrassment, or even secrecy, in social settings but are basic aspects of a person's health. An additional factor related to the topic of sexual wellness is that one's beliefs, attitudes, and experiences strongly affect one's comfort with and approach to this topic. This can be particularly problematic when caring for patients whose sexual behaviors and beliefs are not perceived as usual or acceptable. A key step in becoming comfortable and nonjudgmental when addressing this topic in patient care settings is to be aware of one's beliefs and attitudes about sexuality. Questions such as the following can be used for self-reflection about attitudes and beliefs that can affect one's comfort in discussing sexual concerns with patients.

QUESTIONS FOR SELF-REFLECTION ON ATTITUDES ABOUT SEXUALITY

- How were topics related to sexuality talked about, or not talked about, in my family?
- How were issues related to sexual wellness addressed in my nursing education?
- What personal experiences have I had, both positive and negative, that affect my attitudes about sexuality

(e.g., religious and cultural influences, relationships with men and women, influences of peers)?

- How have my personal experiences affected my level of comfort in talking about this topic with patients?
- How have my experiences in clinical practice influenced my attitudes about topics related to sexual wellness?
- Are there sexual wellness topics about which I have little or no information, or even have misinformation?
- Are there topics that I avoid addressing because I feel uncomfortable?
- Are my views on issues related to sexual wellness (including abortions, birth control, sexually transmitted diseases, sexual orientation and identity) based on scientific information or on biased information?
- Am I accepting and nonjudgmental toward people whose views and practices related to sexual function are nontraditional or different from mine?
- Am I able to set aside my own moral views when necessary so I can address issues related to sexual wellness from a holistic nursing perspective?

ROLES OF NURSES IN ADDRESSING SEXUAL CONCERNS

Sexual concerns that are pertinent to health promotion can be associated with many factors, including the person's behaviors, lifestyle, relationships, health conditions, or stage of life. An important role for nurses is to recognize issues that affect sexual wellness and address the associated patient teaching needs as described in the following guide.

GUIDE TO ADDRESSING SEXUAL CONCERNS OF PATIENTS

All sexually active adults, especially those who have more than one partner, need

- Information about protection from unwanted consequences, including pregnancy and sexually transmitted diseases (STDs)
- Information about signs and symptoms of STDs and resources for evaluation and treatment of STDs
- Encouragement to discuss concerns or symptoms with their primary care practitioner

Adults of childbearing age need

- Information about resources for topics such as infertility, pregnancy, family planning, abortion, and other related concerns

Adults who are around or over the age of 45 years need

- Information about hormonal changes, especially related to menopausal symptoms for women

People who are experiencing problems with sexual function need

- Information about the many causes of sexual dysfunction, including pathological conditions, adverse medication effects, and psychosocial factors
- Encouragement to talk with their primary care practitioner about identifying and addressing underlying causes

Patients who have a chronic condition that can affect sexual function and enjoyment need

- Information about safe and comfortable ways of engaging in sexual activity
- Information about resources and support groups for people with their condition

People who have been sexually violated need

- Support in their efforts to address their situation
- Information about resources

People who have questions about their sexual orientation or gender identity need

- Information about resources to help them address questions

People in a same-sex or domestic partnership relationship need

- Encouragement to have appropriate legal documents in all their health care records
- Acceptance and open-mindedness to discuss their relationships

People who are in the process of or have completed transgender therapies need

- Acceptance, support, and open-mindedness in discussing their gender status
- Nonjudgmental inquiries about appropriate documentation

ESSENTIAL FACTS

Recognize that sexual concerns are associated with many chronic conditions, including arthritis, cancer, dementia, depression, coronary artery disease, fecal or urinary incontinence, chronic obstructive pulmonary disease, posttraumatic stress disorder, and any disability affecting neurological or musculoskeletal function.

Health Promotion in Practice

Encourage patients who have a chronic illness to find information about addressing sexual concerns through support groups or websites sponsored by governmental or nonprofit organizations that provide educational materials related to the particular condition, such as those listed in the ESSENTIAL RESOURCES at the end of this chapter.

TALKING WITH PATIENTS

Assessing patient needs related to sexual wellness can sometimes be accomplished by asking a simple question while providing care or performing an assessment, but at other times, a more in-depth discussion may be warranted. The following guide summarizes general principles and examples of strategies for talking with patients.

GUIDE TO TALKING WITH PATIENTS ABOUT TOPICS RELATED TO SEXUAL WELLNESS

• Ensure privacy and sit face-to-face, if possible.
• Discuss sexual function as a normal part of daily life that affects health in many ways.

- Lead into questions about sexual wellness during a discussion of other aspects of functioning.
- Unless you know the gender of the patient's sexual partner(s) or intimate relationship(s), use gender-neutral words. For instance, "Are you in a close (or intimate) relationship with anyone?"
- If a patient has talked with you about his or her intimate relationship or sexual partner by name, make a point of referring to the person by name if pertinent to the discussion.
- Listen for indicators that the patient has a question or concern related to sexual wellness and respond with open-ended statements and questions such as "It sounds like you might have some concerns about . . . . "
- Encourage the sharing of information by avoiding questions that require simple "yes" or "no" answers. For example, "Tell me about any sexual changes you may be experiencing that may be related to having. . . . [diabetes, a mastectomy, prostate surgery, an ostomy, cancer treatments]."
- Ask matter-of-factly about the occurrence of sexual or intimate partner violence. For instance, "I don't know if this is a problem for you, but some patients are in relationships with people who physically hurt or threaten them. Do you have any concerns about this in your relationships?"
- Don't assume that patients do not have questions or concerns simply because they do not have a sexual partner, or because they are older, or for any other reason.
- Don't be afraid to admit that you are not an expert, but always indicate that you are open, nonjudgmental, and willing to identify resources if you cannot directly answer the question.
- Recognize that patients can sometimes teach you about resources that might be helpful for other patients. For instance, "You mentioned that it's been very helpful to

participate in a support group for couples who are dealing with infertility; can you tell me more about that group so I am familiar with it when I talk with other patients?"

- At times it is appropriate to ask the patient's permission to document information that he or she may not want in the record (e.g., sexual orientation); if necessary, inform the patient of legal requirements for documentation or reporting (e.g., sexual abuse).

ESSENTIAL FACTS

Recognize that many patients welcome an opportunity to discuss aspects of sexual wellness that are pertinent to their health care; at the same time, allow patients to avoid this topic if they are not comfortable with it or have no concerns.

USING APPROPRIATE TERMINOLOGY

Using appropriate terminology is essential for nonjudgmental and effective communication about topics related to sexual wellness. Terms associated with sexual identity and orientation are often misunderstood or used inaccurately, and the following guide summarizes appropriate terminology.

TERMINOLOGY ASSOCIATED WITH SEXUAL ORIENTATION AND IDENTITY

Sexual orientation: One's sexual and romantic attraction

- *Heterosexual*: sexual attraction to people of the opposite sex
- *Bisexual*: sexual attraction to both men and women

- *Homosexual*: sexual attraction to people of the same sex; the term applies to both men and women and is associated more with biologic aspects rather than with lifestyle characteristics
- *Gay*: the term that is usually preferred by men who feel romantically attracted to other men; the term is sometimes used more broadly to include both men and women (lesbians)
- *Lesbian*: the term that is usually preferred by women who feel romantically attracted to other women

Gender identity: A combination of biologic characteristics (male or female) and social roles

- *Transgender*: people whose gender identity, gender expression, or behavior does not conform to that typically associated with the sex to which they were assigned at birth
- *Female-to-male* or *male-to-female transgenders* may be preparing for or recovering from sexual reassignment surgery, or they may be using long-term hormonal therapy as a nonsurgical option

ESSENTIAL FACTS

Attentive listening usually provides indicators of the terminology a patient prefers with regard to sexual orientation. It is also appropriate to inquire about patient preferences for how this information is documented in the medical record.

ADDRESSING ISSUES RELATED TO SEXUAL WELLNESS

Nurses' role related to sexual wellness focuses on identifying issues that affect the patient's physical or emotional health and facilitating referrals for appropriate resources, as listed in Table 16.1. In acute care settings, this is accomplished by addressing the need in the patient care plan; in other settings, it is important to teach patients about seeking help from appropriate resources. Some circumstances require that information is reported and documented, even if the patient is reluctant. For example, when nurses have knowledge about or evidence of sexual violence or other abusive situations, they must follow protocols for reporting.

TABLE 16.1 Types of Resources for Conditions That Affect Sexual Wellness

Condition	Resource
Sexually acquired infections	Gynecologists, urologists, or primary care practitioners
Current, recent, or past experience of sexual violence, including rape, intimate partner violence, sexual harassment, stalking	Rape crisis centers, social services, counseling, mental health resources
Sexual dysfunction	Urologists, gynecologists, primary care practitioners
Pregnancy, fertility	Obstetricians, specialized professionals, support groups
Cardiac conditions	Cardiologists, cardiac rehabilitation programmes
Chronic conditions	Support and educational groups associated with the particular condition
Sexual identity	Specialized medical and mental health professionals
Sexual orientation	Support and education groups

SELF-WELLNESS IN PRACTICE

Take a few minutes to engage in the self-reflection guide on pages 200–201, and consider how your beliefs and attitudes affect your comfort in discussing issues related to sexual wellness.

ESSENTIAL RESOURCES

American Cancer Society
www.cancer.org

American Psychological Association
www.apa.org

Arthritis Foundation
www.arthritis.org

Centers for Disease Control and Prevention
http://www.cdc.gov

Hartford Institute for Geriatric Nursing
www.consultgerirn.org

Gay and Lesbian Medical Association
www.glma.org

National Council on Infertility Information Dissemination
www.inciid.org

National Cancer Institute
www.cancer.gov

National Institutes of Health
http://health.nih.gov/category/ReproductionandSexualHealth

North American Menopause Society
www.menopause.org

RESOLVE: The National Infertility Association
http://www.resolve.org

Sexuality Information and Education Council of the
United States
www.seicus.org

17

Sleep Wellness

Sleep influences health and quality of life in numerous ways because many activities occur during periods of sleep and rest. Sleep-related processes that support renewal and healing of the body, mind, and spirit include:

- *Synthesis of proteins*
- *Acceleration of tissue repair*
- *Slowing of many metabolic processes*
- *Production and release of hormones, such as serotonin and growth hormone*
- *Processing of emotional information to support self-awareness and problem solving*
- *Storing, filtering, and organizing of cognitive information*

In this chapter, you will learn:

1. Physiological and psychosocial conditions that affect sleep
2. How to assess sleep wellness, including sleep apnea
3. How to teach patients about actions to promote sleep wellness
4. Nursing interventions to promote sleep for patients in institutional settings

FACTORS THAT AFFECT SLEEP WELLNESS

Many physiological and psychosocial conditions can affect sleep patterns in various ways, as the examples in Table 17.1 illustrate. Many of these can be addressed through health promotion interventions. In addition, sleep apnea is a commonly occurring sleep disorder that is an important focus of health promotion because serious health consequences can be prevented if the condition is diagnosed and managed.

TABLE 17.1 Risk Assessment Tool:
Conditions That Affect Sleep

Condition	Effect on Sleep
Pain, discomfort, and pathophysiologic conditions (e.g., endocrine, cardiovascular, gastrointestinal disorders)	Restlessness, difficulty initiating sleep, sleep disruptions
Stress, anxiety, worry, fear, and family, social, and occupational responsibilities	Difficulty initiating and maintaining sleep, fragmented sleep
Dementia	Restlessness, excessive sleep, reversal of day-night sleep pattern
Depression	Abnormal sleep patterns ranging from excessive to minimal amounts, early morning wakening
Stimulant products: caffeine, herbs (e.g., guarana) or medications (e.g., prednisone)	Difficulty initiating or maintaining sleep, less deep sleep
Smoking or using tobacco and other nicotine products	Stimulant effects from high doses and sedative effects from low doses
Withdrawal from benzodiazepines	Nightmares and other sleep disturbances
Diuretic medications late in the day	Disrupted sleep due to nocturia
Age-related changes developing during middle adulthood and progressing through later adulthood	Longer time to fall asleep, frequent awakenings, less time in deep sleep

Sleep Apnea

Sleep apnea is the occurrence of eight or more episodes per hour of the involuntary cessation of airflow for 10 seconds or longer. This condition occurs if the muscles responsible for holding the throat open relax during sleep, narrowing the throat opening and blocking the passage of air. People with sleep apnea experience irritability, daytime fatigue, morning headaches, diminished mental acuity, dry throat upon awakening, and frequent urination during the night. Bed partners hear loud snoring punctuated by brief periods of silence. Sleep apnea is an important focus of health promotion because if left untreated, it increases the risk of stroke, diabetes, arrhythmias, heart attacks, high blood pressure, and accidents while driving or at work (National Heart Lung and Blood Institute, 2012). Factors that increase the risk of developing sleep apnea include obesity, male gender, advancing age (beginning around the fifth decade), certain pathologic conditions (e.g., dementia, depression, hypertension, hypothyroidism, kyphoscoliosis), and the use of nicotine, alcohol, and medications that depress the respiratory center. People who may have sleep apnea are advised to discuss it with their primary care practitioner and bring a record of sleep patterns, fatigue levels, and reports from bed partners about snoring.

===== *ESSENTIAL FACTS*

Ask about signs and symptoms of sleep apnea and suggest that patients discuss this with their primary care practitioner.

Health Promotion in Practice

Mr. S is an obese 55-year-old office worker who smokes a pack of cigarettes a day and has hypertension. He reports that he has been falling asleep at work, even though he thinks he gets a good night's sleep, and his wife has been complaining of his loud snoring. You advise him to discuss this with his doctor so he can be evaluated for sleep apnea.

NURSING ASSESSMENT OF SLEEP

From a health promotion perspective, nurses assess all of the following aspects of sleep:

- Patient's perception of the quantity and quality of usual sleep
- Factors that influence the patient's sleep, including undiagnosed sleep apnea
- Patient's interest in self-care actions to improve sleep

Most of this information is obtained directly from patients; however, it may be appropriate to obtain input from bed partners about snoring and other aspects of sleep.

ASSESSMENT GUIDE FOR SLEEP WELLNESS

Questions to assess quality and adequacy of sleep:

- What are your usual sleeping hours?
- When you awaken, how rested do you feel?
- How long does it usually take to fall asleep after you get into bed?
- After you fall asleep, how often do you wake up during the night?
- If you wake up during the night, how long does it take before you go back to sleep?
- What kinds of things disturb your sleep during the night?
- Do you do shift work or have nighttime work responsibilities? (If yes, ask about length of time on and off the shifts, control over the schedule, and so forth.)

- Are you responsible for family members who need help during your usual sleeping hours? (If yes, ask about the effect of interruptions during sleep.)
- How satisfied are you with the amount and quality of sleep that you usually get?

Use the following questions to identify the need for evaluation for sleep apnea:

- Do you experience excessive fatigue or daytime sleepiness, even after you think you've had a good night's sleep?
- Do you snore? Has your bed partner reported that you snore?

NURSING INTERVENTIONS TO PROMOTE SLEEP WELLNESS

Teaching Patients About Health Promotion for Sleep Wellness

Teaching about health promotion for sleep wellness focuses on interventions to ensure adequate and good-quality sleep, including suggesting referrals for evaluation and management of sleep apnea. Many educational materials about sleep wellness and sleep apnea are available from the organizations listed in the ESSENTIAL RESOURCES at the end of this chapter. The following Wellness Activity Tools can be given to patients as guides to promote sleep wellness.

ESSENTIAL FACTS

For healthy patients who have no conditions that require medical attention, focus on lifestyle factors that can affect sleep wellness.

Health Promotion in Practice

Because stress interferes with sleep at least occasionally for all adults, talk with patients about stress reduction techniques, and encourage patients to use these as an integral part of pre-bedtime activities.

Wellness Activity Tool for Promoting Sleep Wellness

Daily Routines to Support Good Sleep
- Maintain the same daily schedule for waking, resting, and sleeping.
- Establish a bedtime routine to promote relaxation.
- Limit alcohol intake before bedtime.
- Avoid foods, beverages, and medications that contain caffeine—including tea, cocoa, coffee, chocolate candy, hot chocolate, and some over-the-counter pain relievers and cold preparations—in the afternoons and evenings.
- Do not use the bed for activities not associated with sleeping.
- Consume foods that promote sleep—such as milk (warm), chamomile tea, small snack of complex carbohydrates (e.g., whole grains)—before bedtime.
- Engage in adequate physical activity before late afternoon and avoid vigorous exercise in the evening.

- Keep sleeping area at a comfortable temperature—usually a little cooler than daytime temperature.
- Use ear plugs if noise cannot be eliminated, but do not block out protective noise (e.g., smoke alarms).
- Use "white noise" (e.g., fans, soft music, and white noise machines).
- If you wake up and cannot return to sleep after 20 to 30 minutes, get out of bed and engage in a distracting and relaxing activity, then return to bed when you feel sleepy.
- Nonprescription products that may be helpful for sleep include chamomile, valerian, melatonin, tryptophan, rose hips, kava kava, lemon balm, and passion flower.
- Avoid using over-the-counter sleep aids containing diphenhydramine (Benadryl) because these are associated with adverse effects on the central nervous system.
- Use a variety of relaxation methods, such as guided imagery, meditation, deep breathing, progressive relaxation, passive exercise, soothing music, body or foot massage, rocking in a chair, reading nonstimulating materials, or watching nonstimulating television.
- Additional interventions that may be effective for improving sleep, when used regularly, include yoga, tai chi, music therapy, and aromatherapy with chamomile, coriander, lavender, and marjoram.

Wellness Activity Tool:
Breathing for Better Sleep

This relaxation activity is designed to facilitate sleep wellness. It can be done as a presleep activity and during the night after waking up when you want to return to sleep.

- Lie in your usual sleeping place on your back with your arms at your sides and the palms of your hands flat on your abdomen below your belly button.
- You may want to place small pillows under your knees and arms to assist with comfortable positioning.
- Close your eyes.
- Breathe through your mouth and nose.
- Draw air deep into your abdomen and fully expel it.
- Focus your attention on the rise and fall of your hands on your belly as you inspire and exhale.
- As you experience the rhythmic movement of your breathing, focus on pairs of images as you feel the inspiration and exhalation of your breathing.

Image	Inspiration	Exhalation
Sun	Rise	Set
Moon	Wax	Wane
Waves	In	Out
Tides	Ebb	Flow
River	Crest	Fall
Snow	Flake	Melt
Plants	Sow	Reap
Hills	Up	Down
Breeze	Calm	Waft

Promoting Sleep in Institutional Settings

In inpatient care settings, nurses have many opportunities to address conditions that interfere with sleep. Interventions that can readily be incorporated into usual care during evening and night hours include:

- Placing a warmed blanket under regular bed linens
- Assisting with comfortable positioning in bed and alleviating factors that cause discomfort
- Adjusting room temperature for patient comfort
- Assessing for acute or chronic pain and offering analgesics or other interventions as appropriate
- Offering warm beverages and a carbohydrate snack at bedtime
- Listening attentively to patients who are worried, anxious, or depressed and addressing needs for information and reassurance
- Encouraging patients to use available audio and visual resources for relaxation
- Using touch, imagery, aromatherapy, relaxation methods, or religious practices as appropriate
- Reducing noise by avoiding staff conversations near patient rooms and closing doors to patient rooms
- Using lowest effective lighting and avoiding disruptions as much as possible during patients' sleeping hours

SELF-WELLNESS IN PRACTICE

Use the Wellness Activity Tool on breathing for better sleep the next time you go to bed, and develop your own pairs of images for inhalation and exhalation.

ESSENTIAL RESOURCES

American Academy of Sleep Medicine
www.aasmnet.org

Also provides Spanish-language educational materials

American Sleep Apnea Association
www.sleepapnea.org

Better Sleep Council
www.bettersleep.org

National Center on Sleep Disorders NHLBI Information Center
www.nhlbi.nih.gov

National Sleep Foundation
www.sleepfoundation.org

References

Agency for Healthcare Research and Quality. (2012). *Non-surgical treatments for urinary incontinence in adult women: Diagnosis and comparative effectiveness*. Retrieved from www.effectivehealthcare .ahrq.gov/ui.cfm

Barnes, P. M., Bloom, B., & Nahin, R. (2008, December). *National Health Statistics Report #12: Complementary and alternative medicine use among adults and children, United States, 2007*. Retrieved from http://nccam.nih.gov/news/camstats/2007/camsurvey_fs1.htm

Beach, M. C., Inui, T., & the Relationship-Centered Care Research Network. (2006). Relationship-centered care: A constructive reframing. *Journal of General Internal Medicine, 21*, S3–S8.

Bisht, M., & Bist, S. S. (2011). Ototoxicity: The hidden menace. *Indian Journal of Otolaryngology Head & Neck Surgery, 63*(3), 255–259.

Blume, J., Douglas, S. D., & Evans, D. L. (2011). Immune suppression and immune activation in depression. *Brain Behavior & Immunology, 25*(2), 221–229.

Bormann, J. E., Becker, S., Gershwin, M., Kelly, A., Pada, L., Smith, T. L., & Gifford, A. L. (2006). Relationship of frequent mantram repetition to emotional and spiritual well-being in healthcare workers. *Journal of Continuing Education in Nursing, 37*(5), 218–224.

Bormann, J. E., Smith, T. L., Shively, M., Dellefield, M. E., & Gifford, A. L. (2007). Self-monitoring of a stress reduction technique using wrist-worn counters. *Journal for Healthcare Quality, 29*(1), 45–52.

Calhoun, J., & Admire, K. S. (2005). Implementing a predictive modeling program, part II: Use of motivational interviewing in a predictive modeling program. *Lippincott's Case Management, 10*(5), 240–245.

Centers for Disease Control and Prevention. (2011a). *Fact sheet: CDC health disparities and inequalities report, U.S. 2011*. Retrieved from www.cdc.gov/mmwr

Centers for Disease Control and Prevention. (2011b). *Physical activity and health*. Retrieved from http://www.cdc.gov/physicalactivity/everyone/health/index.html

Cohen, S., Janicki-Deverts, D., Doyle, W. J., Miller, G. E., Frank, E., Rabin, B. S., & Turner, R. B. (2012). Chronic stress, glucocorticoid receptor resistance, inflammation, and disease risk. *Proceedings of the National Academy of Sciences, United States of America, 109*(16), 5995–5999.

Coleman-Jensen, A., Nord, M., Andrews, M., & Carlson, S. (2012, September). *Household food security in the United States, 2011*. U.S. Department of Agriculture & U.S. Department of Health and Human Services (Report no. ERR-141). Retrieved from www.ers.usda.gov/publications/err141

Conn, V. S., Hafdahl, A. R., & Mehr, D. R. (2011). Interventions to increase physical activity among healthy adults: Meta-analysis of outcomes. *American Journal of Public Health, 101*(4), 751–758.

Cornier, M.-A., Marshall, J. A., Hill, J. O., Maahs, D. M., & Eckel, R. H. (2011). Prevention of overweight/obesity as a strategy to optimize cardiovascular health. *Circulation, 124*, 840–850.

Evers, A. W., Verhoeven, E. W., Kraaimaat, F. W., deJong, E. M., deBrouwer, S. J., Schalkwijk, J., … van de Kerkhof, P. C. (2010). How stress gets under the skin: Cortisol and stress reactivity in psoriasis. *British Journal of Dermatology, 163*(5), 986–991.

Gouin, J.-P., & Kiecolt-Glaser, J. K. (2011). The impact of psychological stress on wound healing: Methods and mechanisms. *Immunology and Allergy Clinics of North America, 31*(1), 81–93.

Greene, S. M., Tuzzio, L., & Cherkin, D. (2012). A framework for making patient-centered care front and center. *The Permanente Journal, 16*(3), 49–53.

Hancock, K., Davidson, P. M., Daly, J., Webber, D., & Chang, E. (2005). An exploration of the usefulness of motivational interviewing in facilitating secondary prevention gains in cardiac rehabilitation. *Journal of Cardiopulmonary Rehabilitation, 25*, 200–206.

Ho, R., Neo, L. F., Chua, A., Cheak, A., & Mak, A. (2010). Research on psychoneuroimmunology: Does stress influence immunity and cause coronary artery disease? *Annals of the Academy of Medicine Singapore, 39*, 191–196.

Institute of Medicine, Committee on Quality of Health Care in America. (2001). *Crossing the quality chasm: A new health system for the 21st century.* Washington, DC: National Academies Press.

Kreitzer, M. J., & Reilly-Spong, M. (2010). Meditation. In M. Snyder & R. Lindquist (Eds.), *Complementary/alternative therapies in nursing* (pp. 149–167). New York, NY: Springer.

Ku, P. W., Stevinson, C., & Chen, L. J. (2012). Prospective associations between leisure-time physical activity and cognitive performance among older adults across an 11-year period. *Journal of Epidemiology, 22*(3), 230–237.

Lattimer, J. M., & Haub, M. D. (2010). Effects of dietary fiber and its components on metabolic health. *Nutrients, 2*, 1266–1289.

Lipson, J. G., & Dibble, S. L. (2005). *Culture & clinical care.* San Francisco, CA: UCSF Nursing Press.

Luck, S. (2013). Nutrition. In B. M. Dossey & L. Keegan (Eds.), *Holistic nursing: A handbook for practice* (6th ed., pp. 261–292). Burlington, MA: Jones & Bartlett Learning.

Mackner, L. M., Clough-Paabo, E., Pajer, K., Lourie, A., & Crandall, W. V. (2011). Psychoneuroimmunologic factors in inflammatory bowel disease. *Inflammatory Bowel Disease, 17*(3), 849–857.

Manz, F., & Wentz, A. (2005). The importance of good hydration for the prevention of chronic diseases. *Nutrition Reviews, 63*(6), S2–S5.

McHugh, M. D., Kutney-Lee, A., Cimiotti, J. P., Sloane, D. M., & Aiken, L. H. (2011). Nurses' widespread job dissatisfaction, burnout, and frustration with health benefits signal problems for patient care. *Health Affairs, 30*(2), 202–210.

Mohammadi, S., Mazhari, M. M., Mehrparvar, A. H., & Attarchi, M. S. (2010). Effect of simultaneous exposure to occupational noise and cigarette smoke on binaural hearing impairment. *Noise & Health, 12*(48), 187–190.

Moore, S. M., & Charvat, J. (2007). Promoting health behavior change using appreciative inquiry: Moving from deficit models to affirmation models of care. *Family & Community Health, 30* (15, Suppl. 1), S64–S74.

National Center for Complementary and Alternative Medicine. (2010, June). *Backgrounder: Meditation.* Retrieved from http://nccam.nih.gov/

National Center for Complementary and Alternative Medicine. (2012). *What is complementary and alternative medicine?* Retrieved from http://nccam.nih.gov/health/whatiscam

National Heart Lung and Blood Institute. (2012). *What is sleep apnea?* Retrieved from www.nhlbi.nih.gov/health/health-topics/topics/sleepapnea/printall-index.html

National Institute of Diabetes, Digestion, and Kidney Disease. (2010). *Overweight and obesity statistics* (NIH Publication No. 04-4158, Updated February 2010). Bethesda, MD: National Institutes of Health.

National Institute on Deafness and Other Communication Disorders. (2008). *Noise-induced hearing loss fact sheet.* Retrieved from www.nidcd.nih.gov

National Institutes of Health. (2007). *Talking with patients about weight loss: Tips for primary care professionals* (NIH Publication No. 07-5634). Bethesda, MD: Author.

Nightingale, F. (1893/1954). Sick-nursing and health-nursing: A paper read at the Chicago Exhibition. In L. B. Seymer (Ed.), *Selected writings of Florence Nightingale* (pp. 353–376). New York, NY: Macmillan.

Oishi, N., & Schacht, J. (2011). Emerging treatments for noise-induced hearing loss. *Expert Opinion on Emerging Drugs, 16*(2), 235–245.

Sabo, B. (2011, January 31). Reflecting on the concept of compassion fatigue. *OJIN: The Online Journal of Issues in Nursing, 16*(1). Retrieved from http://nursingworld.org/MainMenuCategories/ANAMarketplace/ANAPeriodicals/OJIN

Schaub, B. G., & Burt, M. M. (2013). Imagery. In B. M. Dossey, L. Keegan, C. C. Barrere, & M. B. Helming (Eds.), *Holistic nursing: A handbook for practice* (6th ed., pp. 363–395). Burlington, MA: Jones & Bartlett Learning.

Seligman, H. K., Jacobs, E. A., Lopez, A., Tschann, J., & Fernandez, A. (2012). Food insecurity and glycemic control among long-income patients with type 2 diabetes. *Diabetes Care, 35*(2), 233–238.

Seligman, H. K., Laraia, B. A., & Kushel, M. B. (2010). Food insecurity is associated with chronic disease among low-income NHANES participants. *Journal of Nutrition, 140,* 304–310.

Selye, H. (1974). *Stress without disease.* Philadelphia, PA: Lippincott.

Silverman, M. N., Helm, C. M., Nater, U. M., Marques, A. H., & Sternberg, E. M. (2010). Neuroendocrine and immune contributors to fatigue. *PM & R: Journal of Injury, Function, & Rehabilitation, 2*(5), 338–346.

Sorenson, M., Janusek, L., & Mathews, H. (2011). Psychological stress and cytokine production in multiple sclerosis. *Biological Research for Nursing,* published ahead of print on November 14, 2011 as doi:10.1177/1099800411425703

Suarez, A. L., Feramisco, J. D., Koo, J., & Steinhoff, M. (2012). Psychoneuroimmunology of psychological stress and atopic dermatitis: Pathophysiologic and therapeutic updates. *Acta Dermatovenereologica, 92,* 7–15.

Ueland, A. S., Hornung, P. A., & Greenwald, B. (2006). Colorectal cancer prevention and screening: A health belief model-based research study to increase disease awareness. *Gastroenterology Nursing, 29*(5), 357–363.

U.S. Department of Agriculture & U.S. Department of Health and Human Services. (2010, December). *Dietary guidelines for Americans, 2010* (7th ed.). Washington, DC: Government Printing Office.

U.S. Preventive Services Task Force. (2010). *USPSTF A and B recommendations.* Retrieved from www.uspreventiveservicestaskforce.org/uspstf/uspsabrecs.htm

Walker, M. J. (2006). The effects of nurses' practicing of the heart-touch technique on perceived stress, spiritual well-being, and hardiness. *Journal of Holistic Nursing, 24*(3), 164–175.

Walker, M. J. (2008). Nurses' experiences of practicing the HeartTouch technique for one month. *Journal of Holistic Nursing, 26*(4), 271–282.

Wein, A. (2011). Symptom-based diagnosis of overactive bladder: An overview. *Canadian Urological Association Journal, 5*(Suppl. 2), S135–S136.

Yong, J., Kim, J., Park, J., Seo, I., & Swinton, J. (2011). Effects of a spirituality training program on the spiritual and psychosocial well-being of hospital middle manager nurses in Korea. *Journal of Continuing Education in Nursing, 42*(6), 280–288.

Index

Lightning Source UK Ltd.
Milton Keynes UK
UKHW050917251118
332816UK00019B/189/P